Transformed by the Renewing of Your Mind
A radical daily method of Bible study

Jubilee Publishing

©2003 Jubilee Publishing, LLC. All Rights Reserved.
No part of this book may be reproduced or transmitted in any form or by any means, electronic or mechanical, including photocopying, recording, or by any information storage and retrival systems, without written permission from the publisher.
For information: Jubilee Publishing, LLC
41079 Concept Drive • Plymouth, Michigan 48180

PRINTED IN THE UNITED STATES OF AMERICA

Visit our website at: www.jubileepublishing.com

ISBN 1-932314-00-8

1   3   5   7   9   10   8   6   4   2

FOREWORD

I don't think I will ever forget the thrill I experienced each Thursday night as I attended John G. Mitchell's Bible class at Multnomah Bible College in Portland, Oregon. I was a sophomore in college, a business major, but my real interest was shifting quickly to the Word of God as I began to experience the joy of really understanding and seeing it "come alive" as Dr. Mitchell taught it.

Mitchell's knowledge of and love for the Bible captured me. I noticed that the only assignments he ever gave the class were assignments to read and re-read the portion of Scripture that we would be looking at the next week. He'd say, "Just saturate your mind and your heart with the text." Because he had "saturated" himself with the text, and because the result in his own life and teaching was so obvious and winsome, I was encouraged to try to follow his example. As I read and re-read and read yet again, I began to notice a new understanding of the Scripture, and it began to take root in my own heart. This encouraged me to continue to follow his advice and "just read," as he would say.

Although John Mitchell was sixty years older than me and far removed from the secular university scene of the early 1970's, his teaching was still touching my heart and hitting home right where I lived. I could hear and see a Christ-likeness in him that was very attractive. In addition to the powerful way the character of Christ came through his teaching, I was also very impressed with his knowledge of the Bible. It seemed to me that he could quote just about any verse in the Bible that he wanted to, and the Scriputre that he would cite would be practical and relevant to the subject at hand.

In mid-October of that year, he shared with the large Thursday night class his Bible study "method." He said, "I read whatever book I'm studying all the way through 50 times." 50 times! No wonder his mind and heart were saturated with the text! I remember him saying to the class in his gruff but encouraging way, "You read Romans 50 times and you'll be well established."

As a young college student, I wanted to be well established in my faith in Christ. That night as I returned to my apartment, I kept thinking about what Mitchell had said. I resolved to read Romans once a day for the next 50 days. As I began to carve out time to read Romans each day, something very exciting began to occur. I began to really enjoy Romans. I began to understand the flow of Paul's logic as he wrote Romans. I was looking forward each day to my time in Romans.

Looking back, I can honestly say those 50 days were life-changing for me. I gained a new hunger for God's Word, for Christ, and a new confidence that I could understand God's Word for myself. Instead of hop-scotching around the New or Old Testament, I began to feel like I was really grasping the argument and flow of Romans. If this could happen with Romans, I reasoned, it could also happen with other books of the Bible, and maybe, with the whole Bible. This gave me great encouragement to continue.

Soon after that, I began to teach Romans to some other college students. I challenged them to read Romans 50 times. After they were over the initial shock of being asked to read something that many times, some of them took me up on the challenge. They too, found that God's Word is indeed a deep reservoir of wisdom and truth that pays great dividends to those who will take time to really abide in it. Jesus said, "If you abide in My Word, then you are truly disciples of Mine and you shall know the truth, and the truth shall make you free" (John 8:31,32).

In the 30 years since I first read Romans repeatedly, I have followed that same pattern with many of the other books of both the Old and New Testament, and I have never been disappointed. The Bible never fails to yield up its riches to a concentrated time devoted to it. I have had the privilege of discipling many others in this simple spiritual discipline, and so many have told me of the great benefits that they have received. I am confident that one reason this "method" is so effective is that it helps us to obey what the Scripture repeatedly says: "Let the Word of Christ richly dwell within you" (Colossians 3:16). "Like newborn babes long for the pure milk of the Word" (1Peter 2:2). "If you seek her as silver, and search for her as for hidden treasure, then you will discern the fear of the Lord, and discover the knowledge of God" (Proverbs 2:4,5).

I am very grateful that my good friend, Bob Shirock, has written regarding this Bible study method. This book will not only challenge you to give yourself to the Book of books, but will also equip you with some simple but invaluable ways to really sink your teeth into God's Word. You will not be disappointed. God's Word is indeed more desirable than gold and sweeter than honey. I am confident that if you will follow the guidelines given, you will find yourself enjoying the Lord in a new way and understanding His Word for yourself. "Wisdom will enter your heart and knowledge will be pleasant to your soul" (Proverbs 2:10). Don't take my word for it. Take God's Word for it.

Scott Gilchrist
Pastor - Southwest Bible Church; Beaverton, Oregon.

PREFACE

I urge you therefore, brethren, by the mercies of God, to present your bodies a living and holy sacrifice, acceptable to God, which is your spiritual service of worship. And do not be conformed to this world, but be transformed by the renewing of your mind, that you may prove what the will of God is, that which is good and acceptable and perfect (Romans 12:1,2).

The book you hold in your hands contains a Bible study method. It would be wrong, however, to regard this as simply another work on Bible study methods. This book is about *spiritual transformation by means of the renewing of your mind*. The method of studying the Bible proposed in these pages is a means to that end.

Having surveyed works on Bible study methods for many years, and having taught the subject in both seminary and Sunday School, I am convinced that most Bible study methods on the market today fall short in the area of *renewing the mind*. Many methods teach us how to use our minds to dig into Scripture, but they do not teach us how to use Scripture to dig into our minds! And that is really the critical business of the Scriptures and of Bible study as a discipline - spiritual transformation by the renewing of our minds. The Bible was given to us not just as a message to be grasped intellectually. Rather, it was given to us so that the very thoughts of God might begin to grasp and possess us, that our minds might be retuned to heaven's wavelength and our lives thus transformed.

This book, therefore, introduces you to a method of Bible study which takes seriously the phrase, *renewing your mind*. The strategy I propose to you will take you beyond the study of the Bible. My aim is to see that you have a mind marked by the Bible, not just a Bible marked by pen and pencil. I want you to have a mind full of Scripture, not just files full of notes about Scripture.

I am convinced that the ongoing process of renewing one's mind is the key to spiritual transformation. In his book *Renovation of the Heart*, author Dallas Willard reminds us of the importance of a transformed mind in our pursuit of a truly renewed heart and changed life:

And so we must apply our thinking to and with the Word of God. We must thoughtfully take that Word in, dwell upon it, ponder its meaning, explore its implications - especially as it relates to our own lives . . . . We must seek the Lord by devoting our powers of thinking to understanding the facts and information of the gospel. This is the primary way of focusing our mind on him, setting him before us. When we do so we will be assisted by God's grace in ways far beyond anything we can understand on our own; and the ideas and images that governed the life of Christ through his thought life will possess us.[1]

Possessed by the mind of Christ . . . Willard reminds us that we must get back to our Bibles and back to them deeply if we ever hope to experience true and lasting renovation of the heart. The path to the transformed heart is the renewed mind. And I propose that the way to the renewed mind is through a radical kind of daily habit with the Word of God.

The methodology I discuss has a bit of a history:

In 1904 Dr. James Gray published a book entitled *How to Master the English Bible*. In the modern sense, it was not really a book about Bible study methods. He did not discuss details about how to analyze the Bible. Instead, Gray wrote about a process known as *synthetic Bible study*. Gray proposed that the student synthesize or "put together" a whole book in the mind before attempting to analyze it piece by piece. His method for achieving a true synthesis of a book in one's mind was simple: Gray proposed that the Bible student start by taking a single book of the Bible and literally filling the mind full of that book through repeated, daily readings, as many repeated readings as necessary until the blueprint of the book begins to form itself on the memory banks of the mind.

Gray was not alone in advocating this approach of saturating one's mind with the text. The famous British preacher, G. Campbell Morgan, said that he never preached a book publicly until he had read it privately 50 times! Other great Bible teachers of yesteryear, such as D.L. Moody and John G. Mitchell, also shared in a love for the synthetic approach to Bible study. They publicly advocated that students read books of the Bible 30, 40, 50 times - as many times as necessary to allow the book to fully form in one's mind. There is no doubt that much of the great power and impact of these men's public ministries came directly out of their private devotion to the Word. They had minds filled with Scripture, the result of significant time spent simply reading and re-reading the text.

The thought of painstakingly reading a book repeatedly might seem preposterous to us today. Many of our modern Bible study methods books tell us to read a book through three or four times and then begin analyzing. Computer-aided Bible study tools speed the process even further. We can open a computer program, point, click and gather details from many sources in a matter of minutes with virtually no necessary mental familiarity with the actual text of Scripture. Our fast-paced methods are robbing us of something critical - *the renewing of the mind*. We are gathering information quickly, but our minds are not truly being transformed and renewed day after day.

Since Gray wrote his little book, a century has come and gone. I have a newly released book on my desk which surveys dozens of the latest and best methods for Bible study. Gray's synthetic method is not mentioned. In fact, if you survey all of the books written on personal Bible study methods over the past 50 years, as I have, you will find that almost no one is talking about the synthetic method as proposed by James Gray. There is a simple reason for the neglect of the synthetic method as Gray taught it, and it has nothing to do with the power of the method or its effectiveness.

Gray's plan of attack *forces the Bible student to so fill the mind with the Words of God that the mind actually and really becomes transformed and renewed in the process of Bible study*. It was the requisite repeated readings of a book that caused Gray's method to become lost in history. We are so rushed today that we do not have time to read a book repeatedly to the point where it becomes a part of our mind. Thus, quicker methods have pushed aside the slower, more disciplined synthetic method of Bible study which Gray and many others advocated.

You must understand something at the very outset about Bible study methods. A hundred different modern methods can teach you how to analyze this or that portion of Scripture. This is not really the difficult part of the Bible study methods equation. The real challenge is that of saturating the mind with the Word of God to such an extent that this saturated mind begins to govern one's thoughts and actions and change one's life. It is the mind saturated with Scripture that is itself the very best Bible study tool available, and that, quite frankly, is where the various methods part ways.

If you own a computer, you know that it is not good enough to have the latest software program sitting on your shelf above your computer. You must have that program *loaded* onto your computer and *ready to run*. Similarly, it is not good enough to have thoughts and ideas about the Bible on your shelves, in your files, or in some note-taking book which you keep. God's thoughts will not transform your life until they are *loaded* on the computer of your mind and *ready to run* in the daily course of life. The very Words of God need to form in your mind. And there is no shortcut to achieving that result.

Gray's old synthetic method has great power, but the power is in the mind-transforming, repeated, synthetic readings which it requires. Actually, I think this is what God had in mind for us in the first place:

"Hear, O Israel! The LORD is our God, the LORD is one! And you shall love the LORD your God with all your heart and with all your soul and with all your might. And these words, which I am commanding you today, shall be on your heart; and you shall teach them diligently to your sons and shall talk of them when you sit in your house and when you walk by the way and when you lie down and when you rise up. And you shall bind them as a sign on your hand and they shall be as frontals on your forehead. And you shall write them on the doorposts of your house and on your gates" (Deuteronomy 6:4-9).

From the very beginning, I believe that it was God's intention that His people would so fill their minds with His very words that they would literally become walking, talking, living Bibles. He wanted His words to get into our minds and to stay there.

In the early chapters of this book I will be introducing you to the synthetic method which, I am convinced, has great implications in our pursuit of spiritual formation. In later chapters I will discuss a series of analytical procedures which can be layered onto the synthetic phase of study. Frankly, there is nothing all that new or creative about the analytical procedures I teach. It is, however, the combination of the synthetic method with the analytical procedures which makes this book unique in the field of Bible study methods.

I need to acknowledge my teachers at this point. The synthetic method was passed along to me through the ministries of two men. The first was the late Dr. John G. Mitchell, a teacher at Multnomah Bible College in Portland, Oregon. Dr. Mitchell often pressed the importance of daily devotion to the Word upon his students in Bible class. This man's love for the Word was truly contagious!

One of those students was my mentor and friend Scott Gilchrist, who picked up on the synthetic method during an evening class with Dr. Mitchell. Scott, who presently serves as pastor of Southwest Bible Church in Beaverton, Oregon, taught me how to study the Bible while

I was in college. In these two men I saw not only a method but also its fruit. Their lives and ministries proved to me the value of their personal habits with the Word of God.

It is a privilege to be able to write about something that really works - something old, yet something new.

And He said to them, "Therefore every scribe who has become a disciple of the kingdom of heaven is like a head of a household, who brings forth out of his treasure things new and old" (Matthew 13:52).

For Ezra had set his heart to study the law of the Lord, and to practice it, and to teach His statutes and ordinances in Israel (Ezra 7:10).

1

The Challenge That Changed My Life

$\dagger$

Before we discuss methodology, I want to tell you about my own journey with the Bible.

Perhaps you will be able to relate to some aspect of my story. Every now and then someone comes along and says something that jolts you out of your routines and profoundly changes the course of your life. That happened to me.

During my early years in college I made a decision to become a follower of Jesus Christ.   Earlier in life I had *religion* but no *relationship* with God.   During the college years, however, I learned about the grace of God, the cross of Christ, my own sin and separation from God, and my need to say "Yes" to the love of God poured out for me in Christ. Sometime in 1973, I opened my heart to Jesus Christ and began a relationship with Him.   That was the true beginning of my spiritual journey and my interest in the Bible.

> *I was the epitome of spiritual confusion, a babe in Christ drifting amidst a sea of ideas. I did not know what or who to believe.*

As a young Christian I spent several years floundering in my attempts to grow. I had no one to guide me in my new relationship with Christ. Consequently, I was pulling religious ideas from everywhere, becoming quite confused and not really growing spiritually.

I was raised in one religious tradition, while my girlfriend at the time (now my wife) was from a different religious tradition. We were students at the University of Utah, so many of our friends were active Mormons. We found their teachings to be interesting but very different from what either of us had been taught. Then one day there was a knock on my apartment door. Soon I found myself studying the Bible with the Jehovah's Witnesses!

I was the epitome of spiritual confusion, a babe in Christ drifting amidst a sea of ideas. I did not know what or who to believe. Further, I did not have any solid method by which to study the Bible and check what everyone was telling me. Without an anchor, I was drifting spiritually, being tossed here and there by every passing wind of doctrine (Ephesians 4:14).

Then one day on campus at the University of Utah I was given a challenge which changed the course of my spiritual journey. At first, it did not seem to be such a monumental idea. In retrospect, however, this was the greatest idea ever set before me, next to receiving Christ as my personal Savior.

I had found my way into a Christian Bible study group on campus. The study leader, Scott, took me aside and challenged me to begin reading the book of Romans. He actually challenged me with the goal of reading Romans 50 times! He promised me that as I read Romans over and over, he would study the book with me on a weekly basis, section by section.

Now this was something different, to say the least. Here was a man who was not seeking to indoctrinate me into his way of thinking. Rather, he wanted me to become a student of God's Word *for myself*.

He was inviting me to take up the Bible and form my own theological moorings based on the teaching of Romans.

With that bold challenge in mind, I set about reading Romans every day. Now bear in mind, I had never done anything like this before. I had scanned a few books of the Bible, but I had never tackled a serious Bible study project of any kind. I was functionally illiterate in the Scriptures. I actually had to search to find the book of Romans the first time! Furthermore, I was not an avid reader. Books were not my thing. I would rather strap on a pair of skates and play some hockey than sit around and *read Romans*! Reading *anything* was foreign activity for me, much less reading a Bible book *50 times*.

So I read Romans, and I re-read it, and then I read it some more. I read Romans for a week, two weeks, a month, and then two months. I read that book more than I had ever read any other book in my life.

Something, however, compelled me to read. So I read Romans, and I re-read it, and then I read it some more. I read Romans for a week, two weeks, a month, and then two months. I read that book more than I had ever read any other book in my life.

I recall one day, after a heated game of basketball in the gym, I sat cooling off in the locker room. Before hitting the shower, I cracked open my Bible to Romans and began to read. The next thing I knew, I was at the end of chapter 16! This was crazy. I was reading Romans everywhere and anywhere. I was getting addicted to this book.

During those two months some interesting changes began to happen in my life, especially in my attitude toward God's Word. First, I became excited about Romans. Never before had I really grown to love a book of the Bible, but now, Romans was becoming a very special friend. This book was home to me. Its message was becoming familiar territory as I read and re-read it. I began to feel like an insider in the book of Romans.

You know how certain people become fascinated with a movie, a video game or a sports team? They become insiders. They form a fan club. They walk and talk the game, the movie, the team. They are fanatics.

I was becoming a fanatic over Romans! And I wasn't alone. Several of us, all involved in the same Bible study group, were reading the book simultaneously. We became fanatics about Romans together. This book became the centerpiece of our daily conversation. Our motto of encouragement was the three R's: **"Read Romans Regularly!"** And read it we did - over and over and over.

You can tell when a person has been reading often in a certain section of the Bible. The pages start to look worn and tattered. In some cases, that section will start to fall out of the binding from so much use! Our Bibles were getting worn in Romans. Dirt was clinging to the edges of the white pages. Time was being spent digging in the words of Paul. This was the first time in my life that *any* part of my Bible had some mileage on it. All of my previous Bibles died from dust-suffocation! Not this one. Romans was getting some read-time.

A second change had to do with my mind. Not only was I excited about Romans on an emotional level, but I soon began to understand the message of the book intellectually. This masterpiece of New Testament theology was opening up for me. Never before had I gained an intellectual handle on the overall argument of a book of the Bible.

Something totally new was happening in my mind. I began to remember the book of Romans as I read it over and over. The actual words and phrases were making a clear, lasting impression on my mind. I was able to think Romans even when I wasn't reading it. Wherever I was, whatever I was doing, the message of Romans was there, running through my mind like an instant replay.

After the first month of reading, I began to notice that entire paragraphs were firmly implanted in my mind. With just a little prompting I could quote sections from memory. This was very surprising to me as I had never been one to memorize anything. Now, however, I was feeling like a memory champ, something of a walking book of Romans!

A third change came in the area of lifestyle. Since Romans was becoming an integral part of my thought life, other areas of my life began to be influenced by the message of the book. I was just a wild and crazy Michigan kid enjoying college life, primarily motorcycling in the summer and skiing in the winter, in beautiful, mountainous Utah. Yet something new was happening within me. My values, beliefs, priorities, relationships, lifestyle - all had to mesh with the new resident in my mind - Romans! It was as if I had installed a new program in the computer of my mind, causing the operating system of my life to run at a whole new speed. I was not really intentionally changing. Rather, I was *being changed* in response to the Bible as I simply read and re-read it, allowing it to fill my mind. I was *being transformed by the renewing of my mind* (Romans 12:2).

Looking back at that period of rapid change in my early spiritual journey, I think that I was, for the first time, experiencing the power of the Word of God working in conjunction with the Spirit of God to change my life. The writer of Hebrews describes the Bible like this:

For the word of God is living and active and sharper than any two-edged sword, and piercing as far as the division of soul and spirit, of both joints and marrow, and able to judge the thoughts and intentions of the heart (Hebrews 4:12).

I was experiencing the power of the Word of God to change my life *when I allowed the Word of God to richly dwell within me* (Colossians 3:16). Spiritual surgery was taking place and the scalpel which God's Spirit was using was the book of Romans. I was learning firsthand an important secret of spiritual transformation: *The Spirit of God uses the Word of God to transform the child of God.*

The key was that for the first time in my life I was letting the message of God's Word sink deeply into my heart as I devoted myself to the study of a single book. I didn't realize it at the time, but I was in the initial phase of what would turn into a life-long love affair with God's precious Word. I was getting a taste of what the psalmist referred to when he said,

How sweet are Thy words to my taste! Yes, sweeter than honey to my mouth (Psalm 119:103)!

That challenge to devote myself to the Word of God like never before changed my life some 25 years ago. As I look back on the intervening years, however, I am struck by the fact that this Bible study method has touched my entire life and ministry.

THE DEFINING THREADS IN OUR LIVES

Some things come and go in life like passing fads. Good ideas for a while, they soon run their course, expend their value and are discarded. Other things, however, become defining threads - those things around which an entire life is built. What I discovered in this way of studying God's Word has proven to be an asset of enduring, life-long value. It has, in short, become a defining thread in my life.

I ended up having only about one year to learn from Scott, my Romans mentor, before I graduated from the University of Utah with a degree in Business. I married my high school sweetheart, Shirley, and with Bibles in hand and a new found love for God's Word in our hearts, we set out together on the journey of life. Daily time in God's Word became an early non-negotiable for both of us.

We moved to Portland, Oregon, where I studied for a year in the graduate program at Multnomah Bible College. There, I was privileged to sit under the teaching of Dr. John G. Mitchell, whom I mentioned in the preface. I took the Spiritual Life class, in which Dr. Mitchell's love for the Word of God was evident. His mind was saturated with Scripture, and his heart showed it. I will never forget his constant challenge to his students. In his Irish brogue he would quote a passage of Scripture and ask us where it was. We would offer our timid guesses, and he would come back at us with a wry smile; "You people don't read your Bibles!" Mitchell knew and loved the Bible like few men I have ever met, and he was forever challenging us to know the Book and to love the God of the Book.

Leaving Portland, Shirley and I spent the next fifteen years on staff with Campus Crusade for Christ, International. During those years we had the privilege of doing ministry in a variety of settings: on the college campus, in a local church, in the inner city and overseas. Everywhere we went, we continued to study the Bible for ourselves and to teach others to do the same. We saw a pattern: Our own lives grew to the degree that we spent time in the Word, and others matured significantly when they grasped the importance of deeply abiding in the Bible for themselves.

Along the way, I had the opportunity to complete a Doctor of Ministry project on the topic *The Role of the Bible in the Christian Life*. These practical studies confirmed for me the importance of deeply abiding in the Word of God for healthy spiritual formation. My final project was a course on Bible Study methods for my seminary students in the Philippines. Over the years there I had the opportunity to test and try the value of the synthetic method in the lives of seminary students and lay people.

We also had the privilege of living in Aberdeen, Scotland, for three years while I completed Ph.D studies in New Testament at the University of Aberdeen. My dissertation involved an in-depth study of spiritual conflict in Luke-Acts, a theme which I discovered after repeated, synthetic readings of the text itself. It was amazing to me that even at that level of academic research, the synthetic reading of

> *Again and again, in both the academic classroom and the Sunday school room, I saw the value of the synthetic method of Bible study. I witnessed the spiritual transformation which occurs when a man or woman begins to seriously abide in the Word of God.*

the English text was one of the most powerful research weapons available to me.

Returning to America in 1992, I taught in the Biblical Studies department at William Tyndale College in Michigan and later as an adjunct faculty member at Michigan Theological Seminary. Again and again, in both the academic classroom and the Sunday school room, I saw the value of the synthetic method of Bible study. I witnessed the spiritual transformation which occurs when a man or woman begins to seriously abide in the Word of God.

Presently, Shirley and I are entering our sixth year in the pastorate here in Michigan. Our spiritual journey has come full circle, geographically speaking, and today we find ourselves ministering in the metro Detroit area, not too far from where we met in high school in the early 70's.

We had the great privilege of planting "Oak Pointe Church" on February 2nd, 1997 along with 60 other adults. God has blessed us so that today, five years later, we are a church of roughly 1,400 adults and children. Oak Pointe is a Bible-teaching church with great contemporary music and a passion for lost people. As one local radio commentator put it, "Oak Pointe is a church that brings them in with rock, and keeps them in with the Bible." That's not far off the mark!

I've walked you through our spiritual journey for a simple reason: so that you can see the defining thread in our lives. The passion that was placed in our hearts early on - the passion for God's Word - has really influenced everything. Other ideas for ministry and life have come and gone, but this approach to Bible study has determined the shape and course of our lives, as well as the tone and philosophy of our ministry.

Even today, as we teach people how to grow in Christ, we still hold to the fundamental belief that people must learn for themselves to drink deeply from the well of Scripture. To truly help people become strong, growing believers, we must help them to become lovers of God's Word, and capable students in their own right. What we were given at the beginning, we must still give to others today - a way of developing a mind for the Book.

As for Romans, I am still enjoying my good old friend from college days. When I took our congregation through a sixteen-week survey of Romans, it was like going home for me. The themes are as fresh today as they were 25 years ago, and the theological moorings that were put in place back then have held firm against the tides.

I have studied many other books of the Bible in this same way, using the synthetic method of study which I will teach you in the pages ahead. The result is always the same: a growing love for each individual book and a stronger personal mastery of each book's message. And of course, the spiritual surgery in my own life continues. Whenever I allow a book of the Bible to take hold of my mind, spiritual transformation occurs at new levels.

Meanwhile, people everywhere are digging cisterns, broken cisterns that hold no water (Jeremiah 2:13). People are struggling to find spiritual vitality in all the wrong places and coming up thirsty.

As I said, I have had the unique opportunity to serve Christ in a variety of cultures in this world. It has been my privilege to teach the Bible to Koreans and Filipinos, to Michiganders and Oregonians, to seminary students and lay people. Sadly, I must report to you that everywhere I encounter the same thing: most Christians are not satisfied in the area of personal Bible study. There is, in general, a lack of pure and simple devotion to the Book. Mediocrity in personal Bible study seems to be the rule. Meanwhile, people everywhere are *digging cisterns, broken cisterns that hold no water (Jeremiah 2:13)*. People are struggling to find spiritual vitality in all the wrong places and coming up thirsty.

Whatever happened to the sentiment expressed by the psalmist?
O how I love Thy law! It is my meditation all the day (Psalm 119:97).
They (God's words) are more desirable than gold, yes, than much fine gold; Sweeter also than honey and the drippings of the honeycomb (Psalm 19:10).

I believe that God desires for each of us to develop a love for His Word, and to reap the benefits derived from such a love. We can develop it, with His help and a little work on our part. It is not out of reach. The dedicated, fruitful study of the Bible is not reserved for the seminary graduate or the professional minister. It is within the grasp of every child of God. I think we just need to *want it*!

We're about to begin a discussion of a method, but I didn't learn this method by studying it. I learned by *doing* it and by *experiencing it*. Therefore, I think it unwise to simply teach you the Bible study method itself. I would rather have you experience it while I simultaneously teach the methodology to you.

So, in keeping with an old tradition, I am going to give you a challenge!

CHALLENGE: A 60-DAY EXPERIMENT IN 2ND TIMOTHY

Okay, I'll let you off easy. Instead of 50 times in Romans, I'm going to challenge you to a 60-Day Experiment in 2nd Timothy. The exact 60-day plan is laid out for you in the appendix of this book. During this time you will employ every method I describe for you in the chapters to follow. You will read 2nd Timothy *30 times* during the first month. Then, you will analyze the letter in some detail over the second month using methods and tools introduced later.

To begin with, I simply challenge you to start reading 2nd Timothy over and over again. Read it every day. Read it faithfully. Read it like a fanatic. Make it your only book. Put aside the novels, the self-help books, the golf magazines or gardening books. Turn off the T.V. Walk away from the computer. Take up 2nd Timothy and read. Read it in the same Bible everyday. Let the words of Scripture begin to fill your mind.

And while you are reading, pray a very simple prayer. Ask God to develop in you a real heart for His Word during the next 60 days. Ask Him to make you a lover of His Word. It can happen. I have seen it happen time and again in many lives. God wants it to happen in your life too. Pray that God will transform you by the renewing of your mind as you devote yourself to a book of the Bible for two full months.

You are about to enter into an experiment in spiritual transformation. You are going to find out for yourself how truly life-changing the Word of God can be when you really let it get into your mind.

Now get out your Bible and start reading. Put down this book and take up 2nd Timothy. Start getting the edges of those pages dirty. We had three **R**'s for Romans (Read Romans Regularly). How about three **T**'s for 2nd Timothy: **T**ackle **T**imothy **T**otally! Let's tackle 2nd Timothy with our whole hearts. It's a fantastic little book that oozes the heart of Paul for authentic devotion to Jesus Christ. If the mind of Paul gets into your mind, you are going to see some real changes in your life!

2

The Bible and Spiritual Health

✝

By now you have probably figured out that the Bible study method contained in these pages is not for the faint of heart. This is not a point-and-click, fast-and-easy way to gather tidbits from the Bible. This is a method that involves a fair amount of mental discipline. Reading a book synthetically, truly *mastering* a book, will take some work, but believe me, it is worth the effort. Let me begin by making a case for the unique value of this method. Moreover, allow me to let Scripture make its own case for it's life-transforming value.

Four passages of Scripture motivate me greatly with regard to synthetic Bible study. I want you to think deeply over these passages because they contain truth that is critical to your understanding of the Christian life. When you see how synthetic Bible study as a spiritual discipline contributes to your spiritual health, I believe that you will be all the more motivated to invest the effort in this substantial Bible study habit.

WORD-FILLED and SPIRIT-FILLED: A VITAL CONNECTION

The description *Spirit-filled* is used to describe the Christian who is living in close fellowship with the Lord - one who displays an air of spiritual health and fruitfulness; one who is manifesting the *fruits of the Spirit* (Galatians 5:22,23). A Spirit-filled person also sees the fruit of being used in the lives of others (John 15:16) and of being a faithful witness for Christ in this world (Acts 1:8).

The New Testament gives the clear impression that the *Spirit-filled life should be the norm for every Christian.* It should be our common way of living as children of God. We should live daily under the control and influence of the Spirit. The question is, how does one maintain a consistent, Spirit-filled life? What do we need to do?

We live in a day of great confusion over the role of the Holy Spirit in the process of spiritual transformation. My goal is simply to point out one very important and often-overlooked aspect of the Holy Spirit's work in us. Specifically, I am talking about the way in which the Spirit of God uses the Word of God to produce in us a Spirit-filled life. In Scripture there is a *very clear relationship between the Word-filled life and the Spirit-filled life.*

On the next page, you will find a comparison between two parallel passages from Ephesians and Colossians. These two letters were written by the apostle Paul at the same time in his ministry. Consequently, they share much similar content. Apparently Paul had the same broad set of ideas in mind when he wrote both letters, though he was addressing two different local congregations with unique sets of needs. This accounts for the striking similarities between many passages in Ephesians and Colossians.

Look at the parallelism between Colossians 3:16,17 and Ephesians 5:18-20. These two passages, considered together, will help us answer our question about the relationship between the Spirit-filled life and the Word-filled life.

SPIRIT-FILLED / WORD-FILLED:
A COMPARISON OF TWO KEY TEXTS

EPHESIANS 5:18-20

And do not get drunk with wine, for that dissipation, but be filled with the Spirit...

COLOSSIANS 3:16, 17

Let the word of Christ richly dwell within you...

**Two
Different
Commands**

**Virtually
Identical
Results**

speaking to one another...

with all wisdom teaching and adminishing one another...

in psalms and hymns and spiritual songs...

with psalms and hymns and spiritual songs...

singing and making melody with your heart to the Lord...

singing with thankfulness in your hearts to God...

always giving thanks for all things in the name of our Lord Jesus Christ to God, even the Father.

And whatever you do in word or deed, do all in the name of the Lord Jesus, giving thanks through Him to God the Father.

To the Ephesians, Paul wrote that they were to be *Spirit-filled* Christians. To the Colossians, he commanded that they be *Word-filled* Christians. Clearly, these are two different commands. However, the parallel results show us that Paul had the same basic idea in mind in both commands. In other words, *the rich indwelling of God's Word was very closely related to the Spirit-filled life in Paul's theology*. You cannot safely separate the two and talk as if the Spirit-filled life is one thing and the Word-filled life is something completely different. Letting God's Word fill your mind and letting God's Spirit control your heart are companion concepts in Paul's teaching.

A proper understanding of the Spirit-filled life should, therefore, include a healthy emphasis upon the Word-filled life. Maintaining a Spirit-filled life depends upon quality time in the Word. Regardless of where you stand on the more controversial questions concerning the person and work of the Holy Spirit, there can be no controversy about this: the Spirit-filled life and the Word-filled life are sisters. They go together.

Regardless of where you stand on the more controversial questions concerning the person and work of the Holy Spirit, there can be no controversy about this: the Spirit-filled life and the Word-filled life are sisters. They go together.

We must understand that the Spirit of God does not work in a vacuum. The Spirit uses the Word as He accomplishes His sanctifying work in our lives. The commands, the examples, the warnings in Scripture all become tools in the hands of the Holy Spirit by which He molds us into the kind of people He wants us to be.

Neglect personal Bible study and you are, in essence, robbing the Holy Spirit of His most powerful tool to work in your life. The same Spirit who wrote the Book (2Peter 1:20,21) wants to use the Book in your life to transform you into God's image. Our entire theological understanding of spiritual formation (i.e., how growth takes place) must, therefore, include a heavy emphasis on the role of the Word of God.

THE WORD AND SPIRITUAL VITALITY IN THE OLD TESTAMENT

Paul's understanding of a healthy spiritual life was based squarely on his understanding of the Old Testament's teaching on the importance of the Word. Let's take a step back into the Old Testament to see the relationship between the Bible and spiritual health.

The Psalms, perhaps more than any other section of Scripture, speak to this issue. In particular, three Psalms stress the relationship between spiritual health and a Word-filled life.

PSALM 119 - The A to Z of God's Word

The longest chapter in the entire Bible is devoted to an extended description of the value of God's Word for our lives. A coincidence? Or was God trying to tell us something about the importance of His Word?

When you read the mammoth Psalm 119, you come away wondering if there is anything the Word of God can't do. If you haven't read it lately, I would strongly encourage you to put this book down for a few minutes and read through it entirely.

A brief survey of this great psalm will reveal the scope of what God's Word can do in the life of one who studies it diligently. The Word of God will:
  1. Stimulate righteousness in your life (1-3).
  2. Enable you to avoid sin-traps (9-11).
  3. Provide you with reliable counsel (23-24).
  4. Revive and strengthen your weary soul (25,28,40,93).

5. Give you a healthy reverence for God (38).
6. Allow you to speak with authority (46).
7. Comfort you in times of distress (50,52,76).
8. Develop your power of discernment (66,104).
9. Enhance your testimony to others (74,79).
10. Make you exceptionally wise (97-100).
11. Give you peace of mind and heart (165).
12. Produce praise toward God (171,172).

My list just scratches the surface of what this Psalm teaches us. This explains why Psalm 119 is so long.   There was so much that the writer wanted to say about God's Word and the ability it has to transform our lives that he just kept on writing and writing.

If you were reading this Psalm in Hebrew, you would find that it is arranged acrostically. Each of its 22 paragraphs begins with the next letter of the Hebrew alphabet, and every line in each individual paragraph begins with that same letter. Thus, Psalm 119 is a virtual A - Z Psalm, a catalogue of the power of God's Word to change a life.

It might interest you to know that a Psalm such as this was arranged acrostically to aid with memorization. Yes, many Jews in ancient times would *commit this entire Psalm to memory!* They were serious about being Word-filled. No wonder neighboring nations referred to the Jews as *the people of the Book*.

Ironically, they were people of the Book without even owning personal copies of the Book! Few individuals had the privilege of actually owning their own scrolls containing the Word of God. That is why they memorized much of it. They would listen, recite and memorize huge portions of Scripture, beginning at an early age, carrying it with them in their minds through life's journey. They were, more accurately, people with a mind for the Book.

PSALM 19 - God's Two Great Speeches

Psalm 19 is another favorite of mine. The point of the whole Psalm is to extol the virtues of God's speech to us. There are two primary forms in which God's speech comes to us: the Skies and the Scriptures, or the World and the Word. The first half of the Psalm marvels at how God speaks to us through creation, the world around us. The second half of the Psalm marvels at how God speaks to us through His revealed Word, the Scriptures.

Look at just a short section from Psalm 19:7-8. Here, the psalmist delights in the qualities and abilities of God's Word. Consider the following layout of these verses.

The Hebrew poet arranged these lines in beautiful couplets so as to attract our attention to the alternating qualities and abilities of the Word of God. Because the Word has certain divine qualities, it is able to accomplish things in our lives that nothing else can accomplish.

THE QUALITIES AND ABILITIES OF GOD'S WORD
PSALM 19:7-8

Qualities of the Word ◄─────────► **Abilities of the Word**

The law of the Lord is perfect ◄─────► *restoring the soul*

The testimony of the Lord is sure ◄───► *making wise the simple*

The precepts of the Lord are right ◄───► *rejoicing the heart*

The commandment of the Lord is pure ◄─► *enlightening the eyes*

What do I stand to gain from dedicated devotion to the Word of God? Well, go back to what the text says, line by line:

Line 1: If my soul has lost its harmony with God, the Word of God is perfectly designed to restore my soul to proper fellowship with Him. I must spend regular time in the Word to have soul-restoration.

Line 2: In a world of uncertainty, the Word of God is a sure thing. His Word is reliable and trustworthy. It can build deep convictions in my life and transform my simple mind into the mind of a wise man. I need to feed on His Word so that I can become wise and sure of what I believe in a world of shifting values.

Line 3: The world spins the lie to make it look like truth. God's Word is right and true. As I listen to His Word, and apply it to my life, this will result in a deep and abiding happiness, a rejoicing of the heart that I long for. I need to hear and heed the Word so that I can have a foundation for heartfelt joy.

Line 4: God's Word is pure, unblemished, spotless and perfect. It enlightens my eyes to His perfect ways, and it allows me to see the darkness of any other path. I must fill my eyes with the pure light of God's Word so that I can see clearly in this dark world.

According to Psalm 19, the whole man benefits from God's Word. The mind is made wise. The heart is made happy. The eyes are filled with light. The soul is restored. That is the simple, yet profound message of these short couplets. The skies show us the glory of God from a distance, but the Scriptures bring the transforming glory of God into our very being. David, the sweet psalmist of Israel was a man who spent many a night gazing at the skies wondering about the majesty of the Creator, yet he also spent many a day gazing at the Scriptures experiencing the soul-transforming power of the Word of God.

PSALM 1 - The Blessed Life

Finally, let's look briefly at the little Psalm which stands as the gatekeeper to the entire book of Psalms. Consider just the first three verses of Psalm 1.

How blessed is the man who does not walk in the counsel of the wicked,
Nor stand in the path of sinners,
Nor sit in the seat of scoffers!
But his delight is in the law of the LORD,
And in His law he meditates day and night.
And he will be like a tree firmly planted by streams of water,
Which yields its fruit in its season,
And its leaf does not wither;
And in whatever he does, he prospers (Psalm 1:1-3).

Psalm 1 is basically an invitation to enter into the book of Psalms and to delight in God's Word. The blessed man does not walk in the counsel of the wicked; he does not stand in the path of sinners; he will not sit in the seat of scoffers. Instead, the blessed man has made the decision to delight in God's Word and to meditate on His Word day and night.

To meditate means to ponder deeply and reflectively. There is no idea here of quick little devotional readings or five minutes a day with God. The blessed man is one who has begun to devote himself in a serious way to the study of God's Word. In short, the blessed person is the man or woman who has become deeply devoted to the Scriptures.

Notice the results in this blessed man's life. He is firm like a tree rooted deeply by streams of life-giving water. That speaks of strength. He is productive like a tree which bears its fruit in season. That speaks of fruitfulness. He is vital like a tree which has no withering

It is almost as if God offers a deal to us that goes something like this: "You devote yourself to a serious habit with my Word, and I will make your life blessed."

leaves.   That speaks of health. And, in summary, the blessed man, the man of the Word, prospers in whatever he does.   God's hand of blessing is on this man's life because this man's hand is on the Word of God. This is the picture of the blessed man with which the entire Psalter opens. It is the invitation to enter in and read.

It is almost as if God offers a deal to us that goes something like this: "You devote yourself to a serious habit with my Word, and I will make your life blessed." It is not really any different from the deal offered to Joshua and company in the earlier years of Israel's spiritual journey:

This book of the law shall not depart from your mouth, but you shall meditate on it day and night, so that you may be careful to do according to all that is written in it; for then you will make your way prosperous, and then you will have success (Joshua 1:8).

God offers the same deal to us today. If we get serious with His Word, He will extend His hand to touch our lives in special ways.

A COMMON FACTOR IN EXPERIENCE

Many Christians are looking for that elusive "secret" of spiritual vitality. They wonder what is missing in their relationship with God. They are sincere; they attend church; they serve the Lord; they try to live a life that pleases God, but still something seems to be missing. They look for spiritual joy, for spiritual healing, for spiritual growth, but these qualities seem to be the exception rather than the rule.

Maybe the missing piece of the puzzle is regular, quality time in God's Word. I stress that word quality because many people try to read the Bible but see no real fruit in their lives. A *serious habit* with God's

Word could very well be the key to radically changing our mental, emotional and spiritual condition.

Someone once said, *"A Bible that's falling apart usually belongs to a person who isn't."* I have found that to be true as I have observed Christians over the past 25 years. Regardless of what circumstances

> *I find that great men and women of God were men and women of the Word.*

people are in, what trials they might be enduring, or what stage in life they are at, it is evident that Christians who love God's Word and devote themselves to it continually have healthy patterns of spiritual formation. The reverse is also true: Those who neglect God's Word are usually spiritually sick, unfruitful and unhappy.

I enjoy reading the biographies of great men and women of God. When I read, I look for that key ingredient which led to their spiritual success. Do you know what I invariably find in the lives of these great saints? I find that great men and women of God were men and women of the Word.

George Muller (1805-1898) is a good example. He was best known for his great faith and his strong prayer life in sustaining a ministry to orphans in Bristol, England amidst nearly impossible circumstances. Listen to what Muller himself said about his spiritual success in life and ministry:

I believe that the one chief reason that I have been kept in happy useful service is that I have been a lover of Holy Scripture. It has been my habit to read the Bible through four times a year; in a prayerful spirit, to apply it to my heart, and practice what I find there. I have been for sixty-nine years a happy man; happy, happy, happy! [1]

A *lover of Holy Scripture*. That is the common factor I find in the great men and women of God. Some were stronger in prayer, others had a gift of faith, and others a gift of evangelism or preaching, but all the great ones, without exception, knew and loved the Holy Scriptures.

In summary, I believe that the Scriptures teach us that there is a strong relationship between devotion to the Word and spiritual health. Observations from the experience of Christians past and present confirm this truth. Spiritual health and devotion to the Word are directly and inseparably related.

A DECISION OF THE HEART

You have to capture a person's heart before you can significantly change their habits. What I have been trying to do is to capture a piece of your heart, to let you become convinced that you *need* a strong habit with God's Word for your own spiritual health. You must be convinced of that truth before you will overcome some of the obstacles and excuses that keep people from becoming men and women of the Word.

Obviously, we live in the telecommunications age. You don't need to read your Bible. You can have it loaded onto your palm pilot instead of your mind. You can buy the latest Bible-software package and sit at your warp-speed computer instead of pouring a cup of coffee and cracking open 2nd Timothy for the 30th time! There are easier, faster ways to interact with the Bible than the way I am advocating in this book.

I appeal to you, however, to abandon the warp-speed mentality in favor of a bit of old-fashioned page turning. Walk in the footsteps left by another great man of the Word, Ezra the scribe. He made a crucial decision in life. He committed himself to becoming a man of the Word. Listen to the secret of Ezra's life:

For Ezra had set his heart to study the law of the LORD, and to practice it, and to teach His statutes and ordinances in Israel (Ezra 7:10).

Study, practice, teach. That was the commitment to which Ezra set his heart during his lifetime. To take in the Word, live out the Word, pass on the Word. It is no wonder that he had such a huge impact on the life of the nation Israel during one of the more difficult times in her history. He was a man with his hand firmly on the Book . . . and God's hand was firmly on him!

It all started with his heart-decision to get serious about the study of the Scriptures.

Have you ever made a determined commitment to become a serious student of God's Word? If not, make this commitment now, before you go any further in this book. Pray to God, telling him that you desire to be a man or woman of His Word. Ask Him to increase your appetite for Scripture. Confess your neglect of the Bible. Make this a constant priority of your prayer life, and share this need with others.

Personally, I have made Ezra 7:10 my life verse. If you do not have a life verse, why not adopt and memorize Ezra 7:10? Inscribe it on your memory banks. It will serve you well.

AS YOU BEGIN . . . .

1. Acquire a good quality Study Bible. See the section on *Bible Study Tools* (Chapter 4) for suggested Study Bibles. You are more apt to spend time with a book that facilitates your study, rather than one that hinders you. Get yourself a Bible that you really like.

2. Set aside a specific time and place to meet with God in personal Bible study. A daily time of about an hour is ideal. Make this a priority in your schedule. Be consistent for two or three weeks, and you will be on your way to forming a successful habit. A well-lit desk in some quiet corner of the house is ideal for personal Bible study. If you can't carve out an hour, give the best you've got.

3. Look for a Bible buddy. This is someone who also wants to study God's Word like you do. You can study the same book simultaneously and encourage one another in the process. *"Two are better than one because they have a good return for their labor. For if either of them falls, the one will lift up his companion. But woe to the one who falls when there is not another to lift him up"* *(Ecclesiastes 4:9,10)*. Prayerfully consider who you should ask to be your Bible buddy. Ask them to begin this study with you.

4. Begin reading 2nd Timothy. The methods which you learn in the following chapters will be applied in the study of this epistle. A 60-day schedule has been provided which you can follow (see Appendix). Begin right away to read 2nd Timothy once a day. Ask God to increase your appetite for His Word as you read.

3

Synthesis: Putting A Book Together

I study the Bible just as I gather apples. I shake the tree first, then the limbs, then the branches, and after that I reach out under the leaves for the remaining fruit. The reverse order is monotonous to either case—studying the Bible or gathering apples.
– Martin Luther[1]

When we think of Bible study we are inclined to think in terms of *analytical* Bible study: a careful, detailed examination of a limited portion of Scripture, say a verse, or a paragraph. Analytical study is, indeed, a very important aspect of any Bible study system. Analysis, however, must come in its proper place. Synthesis comes first. James Gray explained as follows:

The word synthesis suggests the opposite idea to the word analysis. When we analyze a subject we take it apart and consider it in its various elements, but when we synthesize it, so to speak, we put it together and consider it as a whole.[2]

The aim of synthetic Bible study is to give a student the big picture before looking at the small details, to see the whole before studying the parts. The value of this approach is summarized by Gray.

Like the expert mountain climber, let us take people to the highest peak first, that they may see the whole range, and then they can intelligently and enthusiastically study the features of the lower levels in their relation to the whole. . . Give people to see for themselves what the Bible is in the large, and then they will have a desire to see it in detail. Put a telescope in their hands first, and a microscope afterwards.[3]

SYNTHESIS: THE BIG PICTURE

Imagine yourself walking into an art museum to see a special exhibit of paintings. As you enter the museum, a tour guide offers to take you to a special exhibit. The guide explains that these paintings are the most beautiful works of art he has ever seen. He assures you that you too will be impressed. As one who is quite skilled in artistic observation, the guide comments that "it is the detail work in these paintings which makes them so magnificent."

Entering into the display room, the guide takes you by the arm and hurries you right up to his favorite painting. He presses you forward until your nose is just inches away from the painting and exclaims, "There! See those beautiful brush strokes the artist used? See the wonderful way he mixed his oils in this part of the canvas? And look at this texture over here . . . Isn't that unusual?"

As you ponder the brush strokes, the oils, and the little textures here and there, you suddenly realize that you have no idea what this picture is that you are looking at so closely! "Excuse me," you say to the excited guide, "I must step back for a moment and get the full picture before I can appreciate all of these fine details." As you step away and allow the picture to come into full view, you realize that you are truly beholding a masterpiece. It is a portrait of the face of Christ attributed to the great artist Rembrandt van Ryn. "Ah," you sigh, "what a beautiful painting this is, and what a privilege to be able to examine it in such detail!"

After gazing at it as a whole for a few moments, you move back in for a closer look at the details. Now you can appreciate the fine detail that the guide was so excited about. You are now able to see how the brushstrokes fit into the whole picture, how the combination of oils brings a special light to one area, how a particular detail relates to the overall piece of art. Your grasp of the big picture allows you to appreciate the fine details of the work of art as the artist intended. The original artist never intended for his painting to be analyzed (viewed in its parts) without first being synthesized (viewed as a whole).

When you study an individual book of the Bible, you are studying a masterpiece of composition. The author, under the divine inspiration of the Spirit, created a work of art. It is quite possible, however, for you to approach a Biblical work of art in the wrong way by moving in for the details too abruptly. It is important to grasp the overall picture first.

Synthesis in Bible study allows you to stand back and get the big picture of an individual book of the Bible. It allows you to see the overall theme and flow of a book, its outline and development. Then, when you move in for a detailed look, the small parts of God's masterpiece have meaning and significance in light of the whole. Thus, synthesis constitutes the foundation of any good Bible study method.

Howard Vos captures the value of synthetic Bible study with these words:

...each book (of the Bible) constitutes a unit embodying a primary message, which can be discovered only when the book is studied as a whole. Current sectionalization of Scripture is employed for the sake of convenience only, and it is not intended that the divisions should obscure the over-all message. The book is still a unit and must be studied in that manner.[4]

Vos mentions the current *sectionalization* of Scripture. The earliest manuscripts of the Bible, both Old and New Testaments, did not contain chapter or verse divisions. In fact, they did not even contain periods to divide sentences or spaces between words. The manuscripts were, for the most part, one continuous string of letters. In later centuries, editors divided these letters into words, sentences, paragraphs and chapters, to make reading easier for the public.

EFFECTIVE BIBLE STUDY: TWO ASPECTS

SYNTHETIC STUDY
- CONSIDERS THE BOOK AS A WHOLE
- FOCUSES ON A THEME, OR THE FLOW OF THE BOOK
- ASKS, "WHAT DOES THIS SAY IN GENERAL?"
- GIVES AN OVERVIEW

ANALYTICAL STUDY
- CONSIDERS THE BOOK IN ITS PARTS
- FOCUSES ON A WORD, VERSE OR SHORT PASSAGE
- ASKS, "WHAT DOES THIS SAY, EXACTLY?"
- GIVES A CLOSE-UP VIEW

The point is that these books were meant to be read as units, not to be parceled up into little bits studied in isolation. Breaking the Bible down into analytical units is an important step in the study process. Synthesis, however, must be given priority as the first step.

MASTERING THE BIBLE BOOK BY BOOK

Now I want you to visualize the Bible as a library. It contains 66 books, not just one book. These 66 books were composed as individual, independent units. In essence, the Bible is a complete collection of works of art.

Again, use your imagination for a moment. What would happen if you went into your local library and tried to check out 66 books at once? The attendants at the checkout desk would probably stop you in your tracks. They might even say something like, "Hey, why don't you try reading one book at a time!" And they would be right to make such a comment. Trying to read 66 books at the same time is not the best plan of attack for any reading project, Biblical or otherwise.

> *The best way to master the Bible is in the same manner that it was written, one book at a time.*

The most logical and practical way to master the Bible is not to try to swallow all 66 books at once. The best way to master the Bible is in the same manner that it was written, one book at a time. Of course, there is value in an occasional read-through-the-Bible plan. However, in terms of gaining *mastery* of sections of Scripture and seeing the message of those sections firmly imprinted on your mind, the best approach is to tackle the Bible book-by-book. You should make the book-by-book method of study the bread and butter of your Bible study habit, supplementing this from time to time with other approaches (topical studies, character studies, a read-through, etc.).

Each book has its own style, theme, outline, setting, vocabulary, etc. There is great value in mastering one book at a time. In contrast, there is little value in skipping from place to place in the Bible, never mastering any one part of it. *A good, strong understanding of the Bible as whole comes by mastering one book at a time.*

HOW TO SYNTHESIZE A BOOK OF THE BIBLE

Short cuts often lead to short results. Let me now take you into the heart of this unique study method, and tell you how it differs from most other methods.

There are several short cut methods for trying to grasp the overall message and flow of a book of the Bible. You can open up a Bible study program on your computer and download someone else's outline and theme for the book. Or, you can read a book of the Bible through two or three times and fill out a chart that tries to capture the flow of the book. You might get ambitious and read the book a few times and try to form your own creative outline. Some have suggested that you read the book through a handful of times in different translations, trying to gain a feel for the message.

The fundamental problem with all short cut methods of synthesis is that they lead to *long-term deficits in your ability to retain the message of the book in your mind.* Short cut methods do not truly renew your mind by saturating it with the actual message of the book, nor do they give you an adequate intellectual synthesis of a book in preparation for analytical study that follows.

The product of true synthetic Bible study is that over a period of time *you gain a mind for a book.* This is the key to the synthetic method of study. You grasp a book and you grasp it totally, comprehensively and permanently. The map of the book becomes part of the geography of your brain for the rest of life!

Now, having said that, let's get right to the point of *how* you accomplish a synthesis of a book. How do you put the book together in your mind?

They say in weightlifting, *no pain - no gain*. The same is true for real, fruitful, life-changing synthetic Bible study. *There is really no easy, painless way to do a good job of synthesizing a book of the Bible. You must simply read and re-read the book until you grasp the overall thought of it.* Anyone who tells you something different is selling you short!

G. Campbell Morgan said it like this:

Having read the book, read it again; and in the same way. Then read it once more. After that read it again; and yet again, until you become conscious that the book has made an impression upon your mind; and that you have a conception of its general movement. That is the first process.[5]

I mentioned G. Campbell Morgan earlier. He read individual books of the Bible 50 times before he would preach the book publicly. As he said, "That is the first process."

Select one book of the Bible and read it through from beginning to end, without stopping for details. I have suggested that you start with 2nd Timothy. Repeat the process again, and then again. Don't stop after four or five readings, for the book is just beginning to take shape in your mind at this point. Many fail in Bible synthesis because they quit reading through a book after the first few preliminary readings. Keep reading the book. Discipline yourself to read daily, often, repeatedly.

Have you ever noticed how the blueprint of a house grows on you as you live in the house? Get up in the middle of the night in a strange house and you will walk into walls. But get up in your own house and you can navigate your way in the dark. Why? It's because your mind has memorized the floor plan of the house by simply living in it over time.

When you live in a book of the Bible for a month or more, your mind starts to memorize the blueprint of the book. I suggest that you read the book at least once a day for one month, roughly 30 readings. Use the same Bible for every reading. In this way, the precise wording and even the placement of the wording will begin to form in your mind.

In addition to reading the book over and over, I have found that it is helpful to listen to the book on tape. *Talking books* are a nice supplement, and the combination of the eye-gate and the ear-gate works wonderfully, over a month-long period, to fully synthesize a book of the Bible in the mind. Read, listen and even recite the book out loud.

How will you know that the book is beginning to form in your mind? Try this simple experiment. After 15 or 20 readings, have someone read you a verse from the book. See if you can identify where it is: chapter, verse and location on the page. Over time, you will find yourself being able to identify fairly closely the chapter and verses without even opening your Bible. This will tell you that the book is truly forming in your mind!

Another test: After 10 or 20 readings you will be able to finish verses verbally without even looking at the text. In this way you will know that your mind is memorizing the wording as you are reading. You may even be able to quote an entire paragraph of the book with only a few glitches. Give it a try.

No, this is not a method for the faint of heart or the impatient. Repeated readings give you a clear, lasting impression of a book that will literally stick with you for a lifetime. Be patient about investing time and effort in the synthetic phase. The dividends will be rich in the long run.

RESULTS OF SYNTHETIC READING

1. Synthetic reading has a synergistic effect. When you catch on to this idea of mastering the Bible book by book, something very exciting begins to happen. After mastering one book, you proceed to the study of a second book. As you dig into the second book your study is greatly enhanced by the lasting impressions from the first book. Because you mastered the first book, the impressions do not disappear into a file folder in your desk. They are locked away in your mind via the synthetic study process and carried with you into the study of the next book.

By the time you begin studying a third book, you have gained a personal mastery of two previous books, which now act as a foundation for the third. You are becoming something of a walking Bible because your mind is being imprinted heavily with Scripture through the synthetic study process. Imagine the tremendous resources you will have in your mind when you study your tenth book! The synthetic method builds on itself over time with a synergistic effect. You become an increasingly effective student of the Scriptures because your mind is a more powerful tool for understanding and correlating biblical ideas.

2. Synthetic reading leads to more fruitful analysis. As suggested earlier, the more clearly that you see the overall thought of a book, the better you will understand the details. The small things will become more interesting and exciting once you have the big picture in mind.

Many people try to jump directly into analytical Bible study. As a result, they find themselves studying a mass of disjointed verses and paragraphs, rather than a coherent whole. Synthetic study enables you to understand the overall context of each individual statement in the book. As we will discuss later, *context is king* in the proper interpretation of individual verses. Your grasp of the overall context will prove to be a valuable aid in understanding passages, once you enter the analytical phase of study.

3. Synthesis breeds familiarity and familiarity breeds friendship. When it comes to the study and love of God's Word, our old adage, "familiarity breeds contempt," is patently false. In fact, just the opposite is true. When you spend a long time in one book of the Bible, that book becomes your personal friend. You come to know the personality of the book. Its message sinks deeply into your own heart and life. It becomes a part of you.

Many Christians feel like the Bible is a stranger to them. This is because they have not taken the time to get to know the individual books. The synthetic process allows you to spend extended time listening to the message of a book. This familiarity with the book leads to a lasting friendship. What book of the Bible have you become friends with lately? Believe me, when you live with one book of the Bible for two or three months, it becomes a lifelong friend!

4. Synthesis causes your mind to be filled with God's Word. This is really the practical heartbeat of the method. Scripture commands you to set your mind on the things above, not on the things that are on earth (Colossians 3:2). How are we to do this in a practical sense? Are we to use our imagination and try to dream up thoughts of heaven? I don't think this is what Paul had in mind when he commanded us to set our minds on things above. He wasn't talking about daydreaming.

Heaven's thoughts are found in God's Word. Filling your mind with God's Word (Colossians 3:16) is the most logical and practical way to set your mind on the things above (Colossians 3:2). The synthetic method requires that you regularly read the Bible. Consequently, you are constantly filling your mind with God's Word as you daily read the book. In fact, if you adopt this method of Bible study, and repeatedly and systematically tackle various books of the Bible, you will have a game plan for constantly filling your mind with God's Word. There will not be a day when you wake up and have to resort to the flip-open method to try to find a thought from God for the day. You will have a long-range plan for the daily, deep renewal of your mind.

Let me emphasize once again: we know that the mind plays a crucial role in the life of a Christian. Garbage in, garbage out! If we are always filling our minds with thoughts from television, magazines, newspapers, novels and movies, what good will it do us in terms of living the Christian life? This will only cause us to struggle in our attempts to live a life pleasing to God.

On the other hand, if we are constantly filling our minds with the Word of God, we will be focusing on heaven's thoughts and gaining much more victory in our daily lives. Abiding in the Word, we will begin to see the fruit of a changed life.

The benefits, then, of the synthetic method of Bible study are great. The method is not quick and easy. It requires discipline, patience and tenacity. But the best things in life rarely come quick and easy. This holds true in Bible study methods. The best method is not the easiest method, but it is surely the most fruitful. You will be digging deep using this method, but at the same time, God's Word will be making a deep impression in your mind. The fruit of such efforts will begin to show in the daily walk of your life and in your ongoing ability to handle God's Word.

GUIDELINES FOR READING SYNTHETICALLY

Following are five guidelines, which will make your reading more profitable and effective.[6]

Continuous Reading: As much as possible, a book should be read in a single sitting, without breaks or interruptions. Do not stop to examine details; rather, strive to grasp the overall flow of thought from beginning to end. Remember, during the synthetic phase you are looking for the big picture, not the little details.

Long books can, if necessary, be broken down into sub-sections that can be read in one sitting. Usually, your first few readings in a long book will reveal an appropriate "rest stop." Strive to grasp the continuity of thought in the book from beginning to end.

Repetitious Reading: Repetition yields lasting impressions. This is the foundation of the synthetic method. The more often you repeat the process of reading the book the more thoroughly will its message be imprinted upon your mind. Stay with the book.

Independent Reading: Commentaries and other study tools have a valuable place in the Bible study process. We will come to these in the analytical phase of study. Try not to dive into these aids during the synthetic reading phase. Develop your ability to think independently. As James Gray said:

These (outside aids) are invaluable in their place, of course, but in the mastery of the English Bible in the present sense, that place is not before but after one has gotten an outline of a given book for himself.[7]

Prayerful Reading: Think of synthetic Bible reading as a spiritual discipline performed under the watchful eye of God. Seek to be led by the Spirit of God as you interact with His Word. Consider using the following prayer from Psalm 119 as you begin to read God's Word:

Deal bountifully with Thy servant, that I may live and keep Thy word. Open my eyes, that I may behold wonderful things from Thy law (Psalms 119:17,18).

Thoughtful Reading: A lazy mind presents one of the greatest hindrances to the synthetic method. The untrained mind reacts to repetition by disengaging and wandering. A wandering mind results in useless readings of the text and thwarts the entire process of synthetic Bible study. If your mind is not engaged as you read, the process is useless.

> *A wandering mind results in useless readings of the text and thwarts the entire process of synthetic Bible study. If your mind is not engaged as you read, the process is useless.*

When I find my mind wandering, I force myself to go back to the last verse I remember consciously thinking about. Sometimes that means I have to go a long way back! Often, Bible reading is like highway driving: you can cover some distance and be mentally disengaged. Catch yourself in the reading process, and trace your steps back to the point of last consciousness!

In order to facilitate thoughtful reading of the book, we must seek to involve ourselves in the life of the book as if we were there. G. Campbell Morgan encouraged us to engage our senses in the life of the book:

Let the book be read straight on, and in reading look, listen, and live. Look closely at what you are reading; listen to what the words you see are saying; and live for the time in the very atmosphere which is being created by the reading of your book.[8]

In order to help you read with an engaged mind, I suggest that during the synthetic phase of study you do some research into the background and setting of the book. This will help you to let the book live as you read.

THE BACKGROUND STUDY

Performing a background study is one way to enliven your synthetic readings. The background study is an essential step in the study of a book. I suggest that the background study be divided up into sections and performed during the month of synthetic readings. This will immerse you in the life of the book more deeply and allow you to continue reading thoughtfully and intensely.

A good background study should answer four questions: Who wrote the book?   To whom was the book written?   When was the book written?   Why was the book written?   Another way of categorizing these four questions is to use four headings: Authorship, Recipient, Setting, and Purpose.

Authorship: After reading the book several times, enhance your interest level by looking into the authorship. What can you learn about the author?   What was his life like? His background?   His family? His career? His personality?   His training?   Did he write any other books?   The Holy Spirit harnessed the life and personality of this author to produce this inspired work.   Learn all that you can about your author.

Recipient: After a few more readings, look into the recipient(s) of the book. Ask the same kinds of questions as with authorship.   Try to paint a mental picture of the life and times of the original recipient. You will be surprised how much this enhances your reading of the book. Knowing the life and times of the recipient allows you to read their mail with much more understanding and feeling.

Setting: Then, after a few more readings, study the setting in which the book took shape. What exactly were the author and recipient(s) doing at the time of writing? What was the approximate date of writing? What significant events were going on in the world which might have influenced the situation? Try to reconstruct the original historical setting as fully as possible. (This is an especially instructive exercise with 2nd Timothy.)

Purpose: As you continue reading, try to ascertain the purpose behind the book. Why was this book written? What caused the author to pick up his pen and write it? Why has God allowed it to be included in the Bible? Does it set forth a particular doctrine?   Does it address particular problems?   If the book is a narrative, then you must ask yourself why the author recorded the particular events that he did, as opposed to other events that he left out. To put it in the form of a question: What did this author intend to accomplish by writing this book?

A thorough background study is an essential element in the mastery of a Bible book. Further, it is a good, practical way to enhance your synthetic reading of the book. Sink yourself knee-deep into the historical background. All the while, keep reading and re-reading the book, letting its message saturate your mind.

You will find that during this synthetic phase of study you are become well acquainted with the life of the book. Its message is forming in your mind. Its background is becoming familiar territory to you. Its author is someone you understand. Its recipient is someone or some group that you can sympathize with because you know their situation.

Several study aids will be useful in gathering relevant background information. Bible dictionaries, encyclopedias and commentaries will provide much helpful background material. The historical books of the Bible sometimes describe the setting for other sections. The key here is learning which historical books provide the background for other parts of the Bible that you might be studying. For instance, Acts provides much useful background information for the letters of Paul. The books of Kings and Chronicles provide background information for most of the prophets. Whether you are finding background information in another book of the Bible or in a Bible dictionary, the basic goal is to get knee-deep in the historical setting. Wherever you can find that historical information, get it!

THREE END PRODUCTS OF SYNTHETIC READING

Of course, the most important intangible product of synthetic reading is a clear, strong mental grasp of the book. This is the invaluable result of repeated, synthetic readings. There are, in addition, three tangible (written) products emerging from synthetic readings. These are the background notes, the synthetic outline and the theme statement of the book. You will want to begin a file in which you will save these three important written products.

The Background Notes: After collecting all of your background information (author, recipient, setting, purpose), it is good to summarize your findings. Usually, about half a page on each of the four areas mentioned above is adequate.

The Theme Statement: After reading a book repeatedly, you gain a clear picture of the overall thrust of the book. You should seek to capture the message of the book in a theme statement. Begin with a rough draft of 20 or 30 words, summarizing the book. Then, refine this until you have a clear theme statement of 15 or 20 words. A good theme statement should be concise, accurate, and memorable.

The Synthetic Outline: A synthetic outline is a broad outline, showing the main divisions of a book. This broad outline tells you how the theme is developed from start to finish. It shows you the overall movement of the book. This synthetic outline will be revealing itself to you gradually over the entire month of reading. As you work on and refine this outline, you should emerge with a fairly accurate map of the contents of the book. This is your own independent, unique creation, growing out of your personal mastery of the thought and flow of the book.

By the end of the synthetic phase of study, you should have these three products in hand along with a mind full of the book! These products reflect your impression of the book, gained by patient synthetic reading of the text itself. If you have been patient and disciplined, you will have achieved something special: personal mastery of the general argument of one Bible book. You will have a lasting impression of the book in your mind, one that will stick with you for decades to follow. Believe me, I have Bible books stuck all over my brain, the inevitable result of repeated exposures!

Having synthesized the book, you have shaken the tree, in Luther's words. Now you are ready to reach out under the leaves for the remaining fruit. You are ready to begin the analytical process, breaking the book down into small parts and analyzing the beautiful details of paragraphs, phrases and words.

THE SYNTHETIC PHASE OF BIBLE STUDY

REPEATED READINGS   Gaining a synthetic, overall impression of the book. Filling the mind with the actual words of Scripture. Forming a mental blueprint of the book.

↓

BACKGROUND STUDY   Enhancing the reading phase by getting knee-deep into the historical setting: author, recipient, setting, purpose. Becoming thoroughly familiar with the life and times of the book.

↓

THEME STATEMENT   A capsule statement of the book's central message based on your own repeated readings. This is the heart of the book in just one, simple sentence, perhaps linked to a key verse in the book itself.

↓

SYNTHETIC OUTLINE   An overview of the general movement of the book from beginning to end, showing how the theme is developed in major sections.

THEME STATEMENT AND SYNTHETIC OUTLINE

SAMPLE - ROMANS

Theme: Justification is based on God's grace and appropriated by faith.

Outline:

I. Salutation and Introduction	1:1-17
A. Salutation	1:1-7
B. Introduction	1:8-17
II. Sin: Man's Problem	1:18-3:18
A. The sinfulness of the pagan world	1:18-32
B. The sinfulness of the moral man	2:1-29
C. The sinfulness of the slanderer	3:1-8
D. The sinfulness of the whole race	3:9-18
III. Salvation: God's Solution	3:19-11:36
A. The Law is unable to save man	3:19-20
B. The terms of salvation from God	3:21-31
C. The examples of salvation	4:1-25
D. The results of salvation	5:1-11
E. The basis of salvation	5:12-21
F. The questions of salvation	6:1-7:25
G. The assurances of salvation	8:1-39
H. National issues of salvation	9:1-11:36
IV. Service: Man's Response	12:1-15:33
A. The general command to serve	12:1-2
B. The specific areas of service	12:3-15:13
C. Paul's exemplary life of service	15:14-33
V. Personal Greetings and Benediction	16:1-27
A. Personal greetings	16:1-24
B. Benediction	16:25-27

SAMPLE - HAGGAI

Theme: God's people must consider their ways if they hope to experience God's blessing.

Outline:

I. A Warning Concerning Indolence	1:1-15
II. A Message to Ward Off Discouragement	2:1-9
III. A Rebuke for Spiritual Uncleanness	2:10-19
IV. A Promise of Future Blessing	2:20-23

SAMPLE - HEBREWS

Theme: The superiority of Jesus Christ demands persevering faith.

Outline:

I. Christ - A Superior Messenger From God	1:1-4:13
A. Superior to the prophets	1:1-3
B. Superior to the angels	1:4-2:18
C. Superior to Moses	3:1-4:13
II. Christ - A Superior High Priest of God	4:14-10:39
A. Christ's priesthood explained	4:14-5:10
B. Christ's priesthood ignored	5:11-6:20
C. Christ's priesthood compared	7:1-10:18
D. Christ's priesthood utilized	10:19-39
III. Persevering Faith in Christ	11:1-13:25
A. The examples of persevering faith	11:1-40
B. The exhortation to persevere in faith	12:1-29
C. The employment of persevering faith	13:1-25

4

Analysis: Taking a Book Apart

✝

I once had the privilege of examining a collection of antique cars. The owner was proud of his cars, and he encouraged me to study each one carefully. Pointing to one particular car he remarked, "That one is restored to 100% original condition."

I was challenged to look carefully at that car. The interior looked brand new. Under the hood, the engine compartment was spotless. I crawled underneath that car and, to my amazement, every nut and bolt had been restored and polished. I could not find a dirty or worn part on that car. It was beautiful!

> *The perfection of the details of God's Word can only be revealed through careful analysis of the smaller parts.*

Antique cars look great from a distance, but it is especially rewarding to examine one close up. Only by means of careful analysis can one really appreciate the beauty of such a car and the work that went into restoring it fully.

Similarly, analytical Bible study is that important phase in which we carefully examine the perfection of God's Word. "Synthesis" means literally "to put together." We gain a big picture reading synthetically.

"Analysis" means literally "to take apart." The perfection of the details of God's Word can only be revealed through careful analysis of the smaller parts.

The admonition that Paul gave to Timothy is pertinent here:
Be diligent to present yourself approved to God as a workman who does not need to be ashamed, handling accurately the word of truth (2Timothy 2:15).

If you follow the 60-day experiment in 2nd Timothy you will do your own word study on the phrase *handling accurately*. This is a strong admonition to dig carefully and skillfully as we mine truth from God's precious Word. We must be careful, analytical students of the Bible.

We should model ourselves after the noble-minded students of God's Word found in Acts 17. When Paul visited the town of Berea on his second missionary journey, he encountered an unusual group of people who responded uniquely to his message:
Now these were more noble-minded than those in Thessalonica, for they received the word with great eagerness, examining the Scriptures daily, to see whether these things were so (Acts 17:11).

Yes, they were eager to hear Paul's message about Jesus the Messiah. They were very cautious, however, not to accept Paul's message uncritically. They analyzed the Word of God so that they would avoid doctrinal errors. The only way for them to be sure was to be accurate in their study.

Careful analysis is, therefore, an essential companion to synthesis. Having developed a mind full of the book, the next step is to develop an investigative mind for the details.

THE TOOLS OF ANALYTICAL STUDY
Have you ever had the experience of trying to do a particular job for which you did not have the proper tools? While living in the Philippines, I built a playhouse for our children. I had all the

necessary tools except one; a level. It just so happened that I was building the playhouse on a hill. When I laid the floor of the house I used a pail full of water to 'level' the main floorboards. When the water in the pail looked nearly even, I nailed the boards in place and then continued to build the house

Every skill has its own unique set of tools, and personal Bible study is no exception.

on that basic foundation. When I finished that playhouse, the whole thing was out of square. The roof boards all had to be cut at different lengths because the house was crooked in every direction!

Every skill has its own unique set of tools, and personal Bible study is no exception. As you begin the analytical process you will find it very helpful to have a few key tools. There are five basic tools that are exceptionally helpful in analyzing Scripture.

A Study Bible

There are dozens of different Bibles available in every size, color, shape and version imaginable. Many of these, however, are not designed for analytical study. To facilitate careful analysis, you need a "Study Bible." Look for the following in a Study Bible:
> A literal translation rather than a loose paraphrase.
> A well-designed format, easy to read and study.
> A cross-reference system alongside the text.
> A flexible binding so that it lies open easily.
> A good set of maps included at the back.

Notice what I did *not* include in my list: extensive comments and notes from a particular individual or committee; outlines, summaries, theme statements, etc. at the beginning of each book of the Bible; personal lessons, application points, etc. All of these have a place as supplements to your independent study process. However, I have noticed that people tend to rely on these aids to the extent that they often thwart the process of independent Bible study. Self-discovery is an essential part of both the synthetic and analytical phases of personal Bible study. Therefore, look for a Study Bible that is free from all of these helps. Strength in personal Bible study is developed over time when you learn to think for yourself.

There are a number of excellent Study Bibles available. Personally, I use the *New American Standard Reference Edition*. Your local Christian book dealer should be able to show you many different Study Bibles.

A Concordance

A second very valuable tool is the Bible concordance. This is essentially an index of words used in the Bible with a listing of every passage in which a particular word is used. This tool is essential for performing careful word studies. In fact, many students of the Bible feel that the concordance is the single most valuable tool next to the Bible itself. It can be used for character studies and topical studies, or simply to locate a familiar verse in the Bible. It is a great all-around Bible study aid, and probably the first tool you should have on your shelf.

The selection of a concordance depends entirely on which Study Bible you have chosen. The various concordances are keyed to the precise words used in different versions of the Bible. Therefore, *you must pick your Study Bible and your concordance as a pair*. For example, the following concordances work with the Bibles listed in parentheses:

1. *The New American Standard Exhaustive Concordance (New American Standard Version)*.
2. *The N.I.V. Complete Concordance (New International Version)*.
3. *The Complete Concordance to the Bible (New King James Version)*.

4. *Strong's Concordance of the Bible*   (King James Version).
5. *Young's Analytical Concordance to the Bible (King James Version).*

The best concordances have Hebrew and Greek dictionaries at the back.   This enables you to look into the meaning of the original word and how it is translated in various contexts.   I use the New American Standard Exhaustive Concordance since it is the companion for my Bible. This tool is very helpful and versatile; it has been on my desk for the past 25 years.

Note: Some Study Bibles have compact concordances in the appendix.   These are useful for quick reference; however, they are not designed for careful and complete word-analysis.   These abbreviated concordances usually contain only a small fraction of the entries found in the "exhaustive" or "complete" concordances.   Thus, they are not truly effective word-study tools.   They might help you locate a key verse, but they will not help you perform a careful, thorough word-study.

I will describe how to use the concordance in a later section.   I should note that the introduction of most concordances gives valuable advice on how to use the tool.   Study that introduction and you will learn how to get the most out of this powerful research aid.

A Bible Dictionary
A one-volume dictionary of the Bible is another extremely valuable tool. In it you will find a wealth of information on everything from A to Z related to the Bible.   The Bible dictionary gives you immediate access to scholarly information that you could not find on your own.

Topical studies, words studies, biographical studies, geographical studies, chronological studies, and theological studies are all greatly advanced by the use of a Bible dictionary.   Especially useful is the excellent background information provided on people and places in the Bible.   Again, your local Christian bookstore should be able to show you several Bible dictionaries. The New Unger's Bible Dictionary, The Illustrated Bible Dictionary, The Zondervan Pictorial Bible Dictionary, and The New Bible Dictionary are all worth considering.

A larger store of information is contained in a multi-volume Bible encyclopedia. The Zondervan Pictorial Encyclopedia of the Bible, The International Standard Bible Encyclopedia, and The Wycliffe Bible Encyclopedia are all fine works. Generally, the dictionary will be one volume, while the encyclopedia will span four or five volumes.

Both the Bible dictionary and encyclopedia will provide you with a wealth of scholarly research and background information that will aid in the analytical process. You should have one or both of these tools on your shelf.

Word Study Tools

Individual word studies are one of the most important aspects of analytical Bible study. This is because words are the basic building blocks of thought. A proper understanding of the words used is essential if we are to accurately interpret the author's thoughts. God did not just inspire the thoughts of Scripture; He inspired the very words used to frame the thoughts.

You can look up an English Bible word in an English dictionary. However, the definitions you find there will not give you an accurate picture of the meaning of actual Hebrew and Greek Bible words. It is important, therefore, to have access to good Biblical word study tools in both the Old and New Testaments.

A New Testament word study tool will show you the usage of various Greek words: how these words are translated in the English Bible; how they are used in different contexts; what theological ideas are attached to a particular word; and the Greek synonyms of each word. An Old Testament word study tool will do the same, only the language will shift from Greek to Hebrew.

Advanced word study tools require some knowledge of Greek and Hebrew. But you can do high-quality word studies using tools designed for people without formal training in biblical languages. Take a look at Vine's Complete Expository Dictionary of Old and New Testament Words. This is an easy-to-use, one-volume word study tool. It contains much valuable information and has been of great use to many students of the Scriptures.

A Book Commentary

The last tool I want to mention is the individual book commentary. There are many one-volume commentaries available on the whole Bible. These are of limited value, however, when you are attempting to master an individual book of the Bible. By the time you study an individual Bible book using the method described in these pages, you will be able to write a fairly thorough commentary yourself! The amount of information in one-volume commentaries is too limited for the careful, searching student who is seeking to master an individual book.

I suggest, therefore, that as you study an individual book of the Bible, you select one good commentary on that particular book and buy it for your library. Then, as you study the text yourself, you will be able to interact in detail with one scholar who has also studied that book in detail. Over time, as you study one book of the Bible after another, you will accumulate a number of individual book commentaries on your shelf.

At present, since you are reading 2nd Timothy, you might ask your local Christian book dealer for a commentary that deals in detail with that book. If you cannot find a volume dealing exclusively with 2nd Timothy, look for a commentary that groups the "pastoral epistles" together (1st and 2nd Timothy, Titus).

The major value of the individual book commentary is in verifying your own conclusions. You will not use the commentary to give you all the answers in advance; rather, after you have studied for yourself, you will consult the commentary to check your ideas with at least one reliable authority. This is good Bible study procedure and makes for sound results.

I should mention here one particular set of individual book commentaries that is very thorough, yet also very practical and readable. Take a look at the individual commentaries by Warren Wiersbe. Dr. Wiersbe has written a commentary on every book of the Bible. I have found his insights to be uniformly valuable and trustworthy, combining the insights of a scholar with the heart of a pastor.

Computer-based research tools

There are many Bible software packages now available that package together numerous Bibles and assorted Bible study tools. Some of these packages are excellent. They not only combine the right sets of tools together, but they also increase the speed at which you can access pertinent information. In fact, all of the essential tools I mentioned above are available in software packages. Ask your Christian book dealer to show you the latest programs available. I have The NIV Study Bible Complete Library, from Zondervan Reference Software on my laptop computer. I use it daily.

> *There simply is no substitute for time spent lingering over the text of Scripture, soaking your mind with the very words of God.*

A word of caution about computer-aided Bible study: Do not let the computer keep you from the simple beauty of spending time meditating on the very words of God! This vast wealth of point-and-click information should not rob you of the delight of personal discovery that comes from slow, careful, independent research digging in the pages of Scripture.

I am afraid that over reliance on computer-based research tools can thwart a key aspect of the synthetic method, and that is the lifetime process of developing a mind for Scripture.   There simply is no substitute for time spent lingering over the text of Scripture, soaking your mind with the very words of God.

Having looked at a basic set of Bible study tools, let's look at the first actual step in the analytical Bible study process.

FORMING THE ANALYTICAL OUTLINE

Outlining forms a bridge between the synthetic and analytical phases of Bible study.   As you completed your synthetic readings of the book, you developed a broad, synthetic outline.   This broad outline showed you the overall movement of the book, the broad strokes.   Now, as you prepare for analysis, you want to refine this broad outline to include more detail.   The idea here is to break the book down into paragraph-size units.

Have your synthetic outline and your Bible in front of you as you start.   As you read a major section look carefully at the development of thought.   What are the sub-sections of each major section?   Look for key words and phrases that indicate a transition in thought or a turning point ("Therefore," "So then," "Now," "Next," "Now concerning," "Finally," etc.).   The chapter and paragraph divisions *might* be helpful to you; these are points in the text where past editors have noticed natural divisions in the flow of thought.   In essence, the existing chapter, paragraph and verse divisions are someone else's analysis (breaking up) of the book.   However, I encourage you to refrain from relying solely on these editorial divisions.   They are provided for convenience.   The truly independent Bible student will think hard about where the thought-divisions and transitions belong in the text.   Your eye might see things differently than the eye of an ancient editor.

To begin, jot your analytical outline down on scratch paper or computer screen. After you have broken down a major section, then go back to each sub-section and see if these can be broken down even further. In some cases, rather long sub-sections can be broken down into even smaller units. Remember that you are aiming to break the book down into *paragraph-size* divisions.

The analytical outline, once completed, will be your road map as you progressively study the book, paragraph by paragraph. Your analytical outline will tell you where you are going and the speed at which you will travel. The outline will mark off paragraphs of thought for you so that you can treat each paragraph as a unit in itself. At the same time, your outline will enable you to see how a particular paragraph fits in to the overall flow of the book.

Outlining is an important analytical skill that you can develop. It takes some practice, yet it is an essential aspect of careful Bible study. It is the starting point. You will undoubtedly work through several drafts of the analytical outline. Don't give up! Keep working with it until you have a clear, comprehensive outline of the book. On the following pages are some samples of analytical outlines of portions of books.

After working through the analytical outline of a book, begin *verifying* your results for the first time. Compare your outline to someone else's, either a friend or a Bible commentator. Note the differences and, if you see fit, make changes to your analytical outline if such changes seem to have merit.

Once the analytical outline is completed, you are ready to begin moving through the book logically, paragraph by paragraph. In the next chapter we will discuss how to uncover the treasures which the Spirit of God has buried in the amazing paragraphs of sacred Scripture.

SAMPLE ANALYTICAL OUTLINES

ROMANS 1:1-3:18

I. Salutation and Introduction	1:1-17
A. Salutation	1:1-7
B. Introduction	1:8-17
1. Paul's prayer	1:8-12
2. Paul's plan	1:13-17
II. Sin: Man's Universal Problem	1:18 - 3:18
A. The sinfulness of the pagan world	1:18-32
1. Their great mistake	1:18-23
2. The judgment of God	1:24-32
B. The sinfulness of the 'moral' man	2:1-29
1. God's rebuke of their 'morality'	2:1-16
2. God's judgment on the Jewish moralist	2:17-29
C. The sinfulness of the philosopher	3:1-8
1. Unbelief and the faithfulness of God	3:1-4
2. Unrighteousness and the righteousness of God	3:5-8
D. Summary: The sinfulness of the whole race	3:9-18

HAGGAI 1:1-15

I. A Warning Concerning Indolence	1:1-15
A. The setting of the prophecy	1:1
B. The warning from God	1:2-11
1. The indifference of God's people	1:2-6
2. The command to rebuild God's house	1:7-11
C. The response of the people	1:12-15

HEBREWS 1:1 - 2:18

I.   Christ - A Superior Messenger from God   1:1 - 4:13
     A. Superior to the prophets   1:1-3
     B. Superior to the angels   1:4 - 2:18
        1. Christ's superiority proven   1:4-14
        2. Our need to pay attention to Him   2:1-4
        3. Christ's humiliation defended   2:5-18

5

Unlocking Paragraphs

✝

A paragraph is a unit of thought embodying one central idea. As such, the paragraph is the natural unit to work with when analyzing a book of the Bible. A whole page of the Bible is a bit too much to analyze all at once. A single verse, on the other hand, should not be isolated from its immediate context. A paragraph, therefore, which typically consists of several verses, is the perfect analytical unit.

The original manuscripts of the Bible did not contain paragraph divisions. The Study Bible you are working with probably has paragraph divisions built into it. You could use those divisions to mark off your units of study, but you can also determine paragraph-sized divisions by looking at your own analytical outline. Using the analytical outline as a kind of road-map of paragraphs, you will be moving through the book mining each successive paragraph for significant details.

TWO KINDS OF PARAGRAPHS

There are two ways to perform a paragraph analysis. The method you select depends upon the type of literature you are studying. We will talk about two basic kinds of paragraphs which you will encounter in your study of Scripture. It is important that you develop the skill of distinguishing between these two kinds of paragraphs because the method for analyzing the two differs significantly.

Discourse paragraphs are characterized by very orderly thought, close reasoning and tightly woven argumentation. You will find discourse paragraphs throughout the New Testament epistles, the sermons of Jesus, Peter and Paul, and many of the Poetical portions of the Old Testament.

Here is a discourse paragraph from Paul's letter to the Colossians:

For this reason also, since the day we heard of it, we have not ceased to pray for you and to ask that you may be filled with the knowledge of His will in all spiritual wisdom and understanding, so that you may walk in a manner worthy of the Lord, to please Him in all respects, bearing fruit in every good work and increasing in the knowledge of God; strengthened with all power, according to His glorious might, for the attaining of all steadfastness and patience; joyously giving thanks to the Father, who has qualified us to share in the inheritance of the saints in light (Colossians 1:9-12).

This paragraph is not a free-flowing story; rather, it is something more like a speech. It is tight in its reasoning. It is a formal and orderly expression of thought. It makes an argument; it does not tell a story.

Narrative paragraphs, on the other hand, are characterized by story telling, recounting of historical incidents and a more free-flowing style. The New Testament history books (Gospels and Acts) as well as over half the Old Testament (Genesis through Esther) contains _narrative_ material.

Examine the following _narrative_ paragraph from the book of Acts:

And they passed through the Phrygian and Galatian region, having been forbidden by the Holy Spirit to speak the word in Asia; and when they had come to Mysia, they were trying to go into Bithynia, and the Spirit of Jesus did not permit them; and passing by Mysia, they came down to Troas. And a vision appeared to Paul in the

night: a certain man of Macedonia was standing and appealing to him, and saying, "Come over to Macedonia and help us." And when he had seen the vision, immediately we sought to go into Macedonia, concluding that God had called us to preach the gospel to them (Acts 16:6-10).

The *narrative* paragraph paints a picture. It is not a speech; rather, it is like a miniature movie or story. Narrative material has actors and actions, places and things. It relates events rather than a lecture.

Thus, an important first step in the paragraph analysis process is making the correct call: Am I dealing with a tightly woven discourse, or am I looking at a free-flowing narrative? Since these two methods of paragraph analysis differ so substantially, we will consider each of them independently.

DISSECTING A DISCOURSE: THE PARAGRAPH DISPLAY

The *paragraph display* is used when dealing with more closely-knit portions of Scripture. The visual display of the paragraph serves to dissect the flow of thought between words and phrases, unlocking the line of argument. Basically, the paragraph display is a blueprint of a discourse paragraph. It allows you to see how a paragraph is built, sentence-by-sentence and phrase-by-phrase.

When performing a paragraph display, you recreate the paragraph on a sheet of paper or on a computer document. You take note of the main phrases and show the relationship between modifying or supporting phrases. You note when there is contrast or comparison, when there is progression or regression in thought, and when there is a condition or a result attached to a phrase. The goal is to display the logical relationships between the phrases that make up the paragraph.

In a side column of your paragraph display you will make comments that help you to understand what you are seeing. In the actual paragraph display you are seeking to show the grammatical relationships.   In the side comments you are explaining the significance of these grammatical relationships.

Take a moment to view the sample paragraph display of Colossians 1:9-12.

The paragraph display is a microscopic outline of a paragraph.   Like outlining, it is a skill that requires practice.   But those who master this skill will find that difficult, complex paragraphs of Scripture begin to open up and yield rich truths.   In fact, the paragraph display is one of the best ways to dig deep into the treasures concealed in the precise wording of Scripture.

As a side benefit, the paragraph display will enable you to form good teaching outlines of paragraphs so that you can communicate God's Word more effectively to others.   The logic you see on paper will eventually show up when you explain a passage to others.   For example, the paragraph display of Colossians 1:9-12 might lead you to a talk on prayer focusing on *the one thing Paul prayed for and the seven results he wanted to see in people's lives*.

PARAGRAPH DISPLAY

Colossians 1:9-12

For this reason also, since the day we heard of it (your faith in Christ, v.4)
↓

   we have not ceased to pray for you and to ask...
   ↓

      that you may be filled with the knowledge of His will
      ↓

         in all spiritual wisdom and understanding

▶ *so that you may walk in a manner worthy of the Lord*
▶ *to please Him in all respects*
▶ *bearing fruit in every good work*
▶ *and increasing in the knowledge of God*
▶ *strengthened with all power*
   ↓

      according to His glorious might
▶ *for the attaining of all steadfastness and patience*
▶ *joyously giving thanks to the Father*
      ↓

      who has qualified us to share in the inheritance of the saints in light.

Paul prays for them because he has heard of their new faith in Christ.

He asks that they might be filled with spiritual wisdom and the knowledge of God's will for their lives.

The results of this knowledge of God's will are seven-fold. That they might:
1) walk worthy of their calling as Christians,
2) please God in all aspects of their lives,
3) bear fruit in every good work God gives them to do,
4) continually increase in their knowledge of God,
5) be strengthened by God's great power as they pursue their walk with Him, (note: God has 'glorious might' with which to strengthen His children in their new faith),
6) attain to a level of steadfastness and patience in their pursuit of God, and
7) become a joyful and thankful people.

The transition to the next paragraph is the reference to their inheritance with God.

You will be doing paragraph displays in your study of 2nd Timothy. I have provided samples for you in the appendix so that you can compare your results with my own.   Have some fun with paragraph displays. If you are good with the computer, you can do some great graphic displays that will visually show the thoughts of complicated paragraphs.   Lines, arrows, connectors, color-coding, symbols and graphics from your computer can all be used to great creative benefit. If you are working with paper, you can do all of the same creative work with a ruler, pencil and some colored markers.

NAVIGATING A NARRATIVE: THE PARAGRAPH OVERVIEW

The *paragraph overview* is the second way to analyze a paragraph. This method is best suited for more free flowing passages, such as narrative portions where a story is being told.   Here, the careful logic and close argumentation is not so apparent; hence, it is not necessary to perform a grammatical layout as in the paragraph display.   In a narrative we are investigating a story, not unraveling a speech. Therefore, we approach the investigative process with a different mindset.

Consider again the paragraph above from the narrative of Acts 16. Instead of trying to diagram the paragraph, imagine yourself as an investigative reporter assigned to cover this event. Like a good reporter you want to ask the five big questions: Who? When? Where? What? Why?   You can break these five questions down into three simple paragraph overview categories: Setting, Event and Significance.

The Setting: Who is involved here?   When did these events take place? Where did this happen? You want to learn all that you can about the actual setting because very often the setting will provide valuable clues as to the significance of the event. If you are not familiar with the people or places involved, then do some research using a Bible dictionary, a concordance, a map, or whatever tool you need to find answers to your questions.

The Event: What actually happened? Try to re-describe what took place. This is not merely a paraphrase of the event; rather, it is a description of the event in light of your understanding of the setting. Putting yourself in the place of a reporter again, this would be your capsule report of what took place. In your re-description you may highlight certain elements of the event that you feel that the author was stressing. What seems to be most important as the author recorded this event?

The Significance: This is the vein of gold we are really after in all of our digging. Why is this event recorded for us in Scripture? What is the purpose behind the retelling of the event? What was the author's intent? There may be several significant issues underlying one narrative paragraph. Think hard about the significance of the paragraph before leaving it.

The paragraph overview works off of this premise: Biblical narrative is not just the recounting of history; rather, it is history packed with meaning. The paragraph overview helps us to uncover the meaning which the Biblical writer has packed into the narrative. As you study carefully, you will find theological, historical, apologetic, practical and spiritual purposes behind narrative paragraphs throughout sacred Scripture. These writers were not simply conveying facts; they were communicating to transform lives. God's Word is loaded with meaning!

PARAGRAPH OVERVIEW

Acts 16:6-10

SETTING
Who: Paul, Silas and Timothy.

When: Paul was on his second missionary journey. Just before this, the Jerusalem council had been convened (Acts 15). Some important decisions were made regarding the requirements placed on Gentile converts. Paul and his companions were delivering the Jerusalem decrees to the various churches (16:4).

Where: Paul passed through Phrygia and Galatia. Then, he passed through Mysia and came to the port city of Troas. Mysia is the northern portion of Asia Minor. Troas is in the northwestern corner of Asia Minor, bordering on the Aegean Sea. Bithynia was to the northeast. Macedonia lay to the west about 100 miles across the sea. (The maps in the back of your Study Bible will help you!)

EVENTS
What: Paul and his team were moving through Asia, but the Holy Spirit forbade them to preach the gospel there. They sought to go northeast into Bithynia, but again the Spirit closed the door on them. Coming to Troas, the team was basically cornered with nowhere to go. Then, Paul received his vision in the night. A man of Macedonia was pleading for them to come over and help. The team concluded that the Spirit was leading them to Macedonia, and they immediately made plans to go there. In the narrative, "we" replaces "they" beginning at 16:10. Apparently Luke, the writer of Acts, joined the team at Troas and continued with them for some time.

SIGNIFICANCE

Why: This story is significant for several key reasons. It shows:

1. Paul and his team were sensitive to the leading of the Spirit. They were not self-willed; rather, they were led by God. They were dependent upon the Spirit to guide their mission.
2. The Holy Spirit definitely closed some doors for ministry. These areas may have appeared to be ready for the gospel, but in God's eyes they were not ready. His time schedule for ministry is perfect.
3. Paul and his team were unhesitant in their obedience to the leading of the Spirit. They did not equivocate once the direction was made clear, but traveled confidently knowing that they were in the center of God's will.
4. The missionary team was always looking for men of God to help them reach the world for Christ. Luke was faithful and available, so they took him along as a co-worker. This was the beginning of a lifelong coworker relationship between the apostle Paul and Luke, the beloved physician.

IN REVIEW

Paragraph analysis is a key component of the analytical process. During this phase of study, you are tearing a paragraph apart, looking at the relationship of the various parts, and drawing conclusions as to the central message and purpose of the paragraph in relationship to the book as a whole.

If you have done a good job synthesizing the entire book, you will not have much difficulty seeing the connection between a single paragraph and the surrounding paragraphs. The connections and flow of thought which you detected during the synthetic phase will only be magnified under the investigative lens of the paragraph analysis. Again, synthesis and analysis are two aspects of the Bible study process which must work together.

Two kinds of paragraphs were discussed: the narrative paragraph and the discourse paragraph. The narrative paragraph, being more free flowing and story-like, calls for a paragraph overview, navigating the who, when, where, what and why of the story. The discourse paragraph, being more tightly woven and speech-like, calls for a paragraph display, unlocking the close logic and argumentation that build the main ideas of the paragraph line upon line.

As you examine paragraphs closely, you will undoubtedly encounter individual words and phrases that warrant more careful study, leading us to the next step in the analytical process: the word study.

6

The Power of Words

$$\dagger$$

"Do not think that I came to abolish the Law or the Prophets; I did not come to abolish, but to fulfill. For truly I say to you, until heaven and earth pass away, not the smallest letter or stroke shall pass away from the Law, until all is accomplished" (Matthew 5:17,18).

Not the smallest letter or stroke . . . Jesus was referring to the smallest stroke of the Hebrew scribe's pen, as in the letter *yodh* (י). Scripture is inspired down to the very details of the words chosen by the Spirit of God! That is why it is so important in our analysis of Scripture to dig right down to the level of the precise wording. The Spirit was not careless in producing the very words of Scripture, nor should we be careless in studying the precise language.

Individual biblical words, when rightly understood, have tremendous power to transform our minds and shape our lives. Often you will find a great insight in the meaning of a single word. I have done individual word studies that have stayed in my mind and shaped my thinking for decades.

But why do we need to *study* biblical words? Can we not simply rely on the obvious meanings of the English words in our translation of the

Bible? Indeed, most often the simple meaning of a Hebrew (Old Testament) or Greek (New Testament) word will be conveyed effectively in the English equivalent in a carefully prepared translation. Thus, a clear understanding of the meaning of the English word is usually sufficient. Sometimes, however, there is richer meaning to be discovered *behind* the English equivalent, in the original meaning of the Hebrew or Greek word. In order to discover that richer treasure of meaning you must develop some skill in word studies.

TWO APPROACHES TO WORD STUDIES

I gave you two different methods for analyzing paragraphs. Now let me introduce you to two different kinds of word studies. The kind of word study you perform depends upon the kind of word you are looking at. So again, the starting point is to make an informed decision about a word.

Consider the following two lists of words and phrases taken from 2nd Timothy.

DESCRIPTIVE WORDS	TOPICAL WORDS
clear	soldier
sincere	athlete
kindle afresh	farmer
ashamed	drink offering
convinced	gold vessel
diligent	wood vessel
handling accurately	bond-servant
inspired	kingdom
equipped	crown
perseverance	parchments
reprove	coppersmith

DESCRIPTIVE WORDS
rebuke
exhort
guard

TOPICAL WORDS
Demas
Onesiphorus
Troas

Notice that the words in the left column are basically all verbs of action or modifiers. I call them *descriptive* words because they are used to modify or describe people, objects and actions. They attribute qualities or characteristics to things, or they issue verbal commands to do things in a certain way.

Now compare these with the words in the right column. Each of these words is really a *topic* in itself. These are people, places and things; they are tangible or touchable. You can touch a *crown* or a *farmer* or a *drinking vessel*. But it would be hard to put your hand on a *sincere* or a *diligent* or a *rebuke*. So, there are words that *embody things* (topical words) and there are other words that *describe things* (descriptive words).

Notice the descriptive (D) and topical (T) words in the following sentences:

The <u>hard-working</u> (D) <u>farmer</u> (T) ought to be the first to receive his share of the <u>crops</u> (T). <u>Consider</u> (D) what I say, for the Lord will give you <u>understanding</u> (D) in everything (2Tim. 2:6,7).

Now when Jesus was in <u>Bethany</u> (T), at the home of Simon the leper (T), a woman came to Him with an <u>alabaster vial</u> (T) of <u>very costly</u> (D) <u>perfume</u> (T), and she poured it upon His head as He <u>reclined</u> (D) at the <u>table</u> (T) (Matthew 26:6,7).

Now the methods for studying the two kinds of words are different. If you employ the exact same procedure for the words *reprove* and *coppersmith* you will not come up with good results. In the case of the word *reprove*, you are interested in determining *the meaning and force* of the action being described. With the word *coppersmith*, on the other hand, you are more interested in the *background and practice* of a coppersmith. You must learn to use the word-study method that is appropriate for the kind of word you are investigating.

SELECTING WORDS TO STUDY
When you dig for gold, the first step is to know where to dig! The place to start a word study is to select the best words to analyze. You have a paragraph overview or a paragraph display sitting in front of you. As you scan that paragraph you must ask yourself: What are the most significant individual words and phrases here?

> *As you scan that paragraph you must ask yourself: What are the most significant individual words and phrases here?*

Which words make the most difference in my understanding of the passage? Which words are most interesting?

Below are two selections from 2nd Timothy, the first from a discourse section and the second from a more narrative-like section. In each selection I have underlined words and phrases that would seem to have potential for interesting word studies. Again, I have classified the words as either descriptive (D) or topical (T).   Study carefully these two selections.

Discourse:
Nevertheless, the <u>firm foundation</u> (D) of God stands, having this <u>seal</u> (T), "The Lord knows those who are His," and, "Let everyone who names the name of the Lord <u>abstain</u> (D) from <u>wickedness</u> (D)." Now in a large house there are not only <u>gold and silver vessels</u> (T), but also <u>vessels of wood and of earthenware</u> (T), and some to <u>honor</u> (D) and some to <u>dishonor</u> (D). Therefore, if a man <u>cleanses</u> (D)

himself from these things, he will be a vessel for honor, <u>sanctified</u> (D), useful to the Master, <u>prepared</u> (D) for every good work (2Timothy 2:19-21).

Narrative:

Make every <u>effort</u> (D) to come to me soon; for <u>Demas</u> (T), having <u>loved</u> (D) this present world, has <u>deserted</u> (D) me and gone to <u>Thessalonica</u> (T); <u>Crescens</u> (T) has gone to <u>Galatia</u> (T), <u>Titus</u> (T) to <u>Dalmatia</u> (T). Only <u>Luke</u> (T) is with me. Pick up <u>Mark</u> (T) and bring him with you, for he is <u>useful</u> (D) to me for service. But <u>Tychicus</u> (T) I have sent to <u>Ephesus</u> (T). When you come bring the <u>cloak</u> (T) which I left at <u>Troas</u> (T) with <u>Carpus</u> (T), and the <u>books</u> (T), especially the <u>parchments</u> (T) (2Timothy 4:9-13).

Notice that there were more descriptive (D) words than topical words in the discourse paragraph (2Timothy 2:19-21). That is very common due to the nature of the language in discourse. On the other hand, you will very often find a greater number of topical (T) words in a narrative-type paragraph in which a story is being told involving people, places and things. The sample from 2nd Timothy 4:9-13 abounds with topical words. You will, over time, become accustomed to the distribution of descriptive and topical words in the various portions of Scripture.

Depending upon the amount of time you have, it may be necessary to limit the number of words you choose to study. For example, in the selection from 2Timothy 4:9-13 there are fifteen different topical (T) words to investigate! Certainly, all of these words have value, but in the face of so many good possibilities, you must become selective. What topical words in this particular selection have the most potential for opening up your understanding of 2nd Timothy? I would probably choose the following topical words for analysis: *Demas, Luke, Mark, books* and *parchments.* I might add all four descriptive words: *effort, loved*, *deserted* and *useful*. I am confident that these nine words will open up many great avenues for a deeper understanding of Paul's message in 2nd Timothy.

The previous discourse selection from 2Timothy 2:19-21 had eight descriptive (D) words and three topical (T) words of interest. Given the central thrust of this section, I would probably limit my word studies to these descriptive words: *wickedness, honor, dishonor, cleanses, sanctified* and *prepared*. In addition, I would study these topical phrases: *gold and silver vessels, wood* and *earthenware vessels*. By focusing on these words, I will dig out the meaning of Paul in this selection and come away with valuable insights that will stick with me for a lifetime.

> *To become proficient in selecting good words is simple: start doing word studies! The more you study words, the sharper you become in picking out significant words to study.*

Learning to select and classify words, then, is the starting point for word study. To become proficient in selecting good words is simple: start doing word studies! The more you study words, the sharper you become in picking out significant words to study. Like all of Bible study, it is a skill that develops with practice.

Having selected some descriptive (D) and topical (T) words, you should enter upon one of the following word-study procedures.

THE TOPICAL WORD STUDY
Tools Needed: Bible Dictionary and/or Encyclopedia

We'll start by discussing the topical word study since it is the easiest to perform. In essence, a topical word leads you into a miniature background study. You are looking behind the scenes into the Biblical world by examining objects, people, places and things as they appear in individual words.

For example, in 2nd Timothy I encounter topical words like: *farmer, soldier, vessel, drink offering, Demas, books, parchments, etc.* I am interested in the background of these words, so I ask myself questions such as:

- What was a *farmer* like in Paul's day? How did farming activity differ from farming today?
- What was the routine of a *soldier* in the Roman army? What was their training, discipline, etc?
- What were *gold and silver vessels* used for in homes? What about *wood and earthenware vessels*?
- What is the significance of a *drink offering*? Why does Paul describe his life with this figure?
- Who was *Demas* and what was his connection with Paul? Why did he desert Paul in the end?
- What were *parchments* and how do these differ from *books*? Why did Paul request these things?

The topical word study is relatively simple to perform. The Bible dictionary or encyclopedia will do most of the work for you. These books are gold mines of information on every topic in the Bible. You simply need to find the page that deals with your topic and dig in!

Finding the relevant information in the Bible dictionary might require some snooping around. You usually have to come up with some parallel topics in order to hit the jackpot. For example, here is the process I went through to find information on several topical words in a Bible dictionary:

Athlete
- Looked up *Athletics* and found nothing.
- Looked up *Competition* and found nothing.
- Looked up *Sports* and was referred to *Games*.
- Looked up *Games* and found a full page of information.

Soldier
- Looked up *Soldier* and found nothing.
- Looked up *Army* and found one page. Was referred to *War* for more information.
- Looked up *War* and found another full page of information.

Farmer
- Looked up *Farmer* and found nothing.
- Looked up *Farm* and was referred to *Agriculture*.
- Looked up *Agriculture* and found two pages of information.

Essentially, the topical word study is a treasure hunt. The treasure is in the Bible dictionary and/or encyclopedia. Once you find it, your understanding of the passage will be greatly enriched as you immerse yourself in the life and times of the Biblical writers via the study of an individual word.

> **Essentially, the topical word study is a treasure hunt. The treasure is in the Bible dictionary and/or encyclopedia.**

After you have studied the topical word in some detail, go back to the passage of the Bible you are analyzing and apply your research to obtain a richer and fuller understanding of the author's message. You will be amazed at what lies beneath the surface of the topical language in Scripture.

THE DESCRIPTIVE WORD STUDY

Tools Needed: Concordance, Word-Study Book, Commentary.

The descriptive word study requires more skill than the topical word study. In the study of a descriptive word, you are looking for the *meaning and force* of the word *in a particular context*. The same word might have slightly different shades of meaning in differing contexts. So the idea with a descriptive word is to proceed from general to specific.   First, you seek to understand the general usage of a word by seeing how it is used in a variety of contexts. Second, you go back to your particular passage and determine how the word is being used in the immediate context.

Descriptive Word

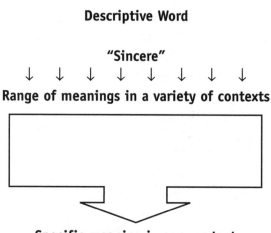

"Sincere"

↓   ↓   ↓   ↓   ↓   ↓   ↓   ↓

Range of meanings in a variety of contexts

Specific meaning in one context

The quick way to do a descriptive word study is to consult a tool such as *Vine's Expository Dictionary of Old and New Testament Words.* There, you will find a complete word study on the *general usage* of a word already done for you. The tool will show you the range of possible meanings in a variety of contexts. After reading the entry in the tool, and seeing the range of meanings for your word, you take this information and apply it to your particular passage.

One word of caution: When you see the range of possible meanings for your word, you must resist the urge to pick any meaning that you like best and apply it to your passage. This is one of the great errors of word study that Bible students often commit. Instead, you must take the range of possible meanings, go back to your specific context, and see how the various definitions fit *in context*. The idea is *not* to pick the definition which you like the best, or the one which lends the most creative slant to the passage; rather, the idea is to *pick the definition which fits the immediate context most naturally*. You want to know what the author really meant, and this requires careful thought.

Often a good commentary will prove its value at this point. Detailed commentaries provide an opinion on the meaning of key words and phrases in the context of that particular book of the Bible. This is a key reason to use a quality commentary to verify your own thinking about the meaning of a word in a particular passage of Scripture. Occasionally, the word-study tool, like *Vine's*, will discuss the meaning of your particular word in the specific passage which you are studying.

Again, this is the quick way to do a descriptive word study. Using the word-study tool and the commentary, you should be able to arrive at some rapid, accurate results for descriptive words.

The longer method for descriptive word studies takes you even deeper. This procedure involves the use of the concordance. Instead of relying on the research of someone else to give you the range of possible meanings, you can do the homework for yourself. Here are the steps involved:

First, you must locate numerous passages where your word is used by looking in the main body of the concordance. Some words are used only a few times. Other words might be used hundreds of times. Note: You must be sure that you are actually looking at the *same original Greek or Hebrew word* in the various passages. You can determine this *by looking at the numbering system used in conjunction with each word*. This is important because you are not studying an English word; rather, you are studying what was originally a Greek or Hebrew word. It is, therefore, essential to make sure that you are looking at passages that use your Greek or Hebrew word specifically. (Reminder: The instructions at the beginning of the concordance are very valuable in showing you how to use this tool properly.)

Second, having located passages that use your particular word, you must open up your Bible and look up many of these passages and see how the word actually is used in various contexts. As you see how the word is used in a variety of contexts, you will form an idea of the *general usage* of the word (a set of potential definitions). You are doing what the word-study tools did for you - determining the range of possible meanings of a word. (Hint: The computer-aided study packages become very valuable at this point, as they allow you to scroll through passages quickly, based on word searches.)

Third, having gained a sense for the range of possible meanings, you return to your original context in the book you are studying. As you apply your research to your particular passage, you will be able to select the specific meaning which is best suited to that context.

In this more time-consuming method, you are adding the step of doing in-depth research for yourself into the wider range of meanings, instead of simply relying on the experts. The benefit of this more arduous approach is that it takes you deeper into the language of the Bible for yourself. Once again, you can *verify* your results by checking with both the word-study tool and the commentary.

> *Good theology grows out of careful descriptive word studies. It is not uncommon to find an important doctrine hinging upon the specific contextual meaning of a single descriptive word.*

Although it sounds quite involved, this longer method of word study does not really take too much time when you are dealing with words that are used less than a dozen times in the Old or New Testament. You can locate the words quickly with the concordance, and spend a few more minutes reading the various passages.   You will gain valuable insight from this kind of word searching.

Good theology grows out of careful descriptive word studies. It is not uncommon to find an important doctrine hinging upon the specific contextual meaning of a single descriptive word. Therefore, though the descriptive word study is more difficult than the topical word study, I urge you to be diligent and careful in the study of descriptive words.

SUMMARY

There are no wasted letters or strokes in Scripture. The Holy Spirit inspired the very choice of words.   While our English translations provide a good basic understanding of word meanings, much can be gained from careful, thoughtful research into the original biblical words. The topical word study involves a treasure hunt in the Bible dictionary or encyclopedia. The descriptive word study requires a wide-angle look at the general usage and meaning of a word in various contexts, followed by a narrowing of the lens to look at the specific contextual meaning.

There is rich reward in the study of both kinds of words. Good word studies will also enable you to better communicate God's truth to others.   Work at it!   It is worth the effort.   I conclude this chapter with a handful of random samples.   Take some time to ponder these before you move on.

SAMPLE WORD STUDIES

COMFORT - 2Corinthians 1:3-7 (Descriptive word)
General usage: This word occurs more in 2Corinthians than in any other N.T. book (1:3,4,5,6,7; 2:7; 7:4,6,7,13;13:11). The Greek word is _paraklesis_, derived from the verb _parakaleo_ (para = by the side of, and kaleo = to call). Hence, _parakaleo_ means "to call to one's side" and has the idea of "encouragement." The noun _parakiesis_ means: a calling to one's aid, encouragement. This word is translated "comfort," "encouragement," "exhortation" and "consolation."

This same root word is used to describe the Holy Spirit as our personal "Helper" (_parakletos_ - John 14:16,26;15:26;16:7). The idea is that of one who comes alongside to assist us.

Usage in context: The "comfort" that Paul speaks of in 2Corinthians 1:3-7 is that supernatural encouragement or consolation that the God of all comfort gives to His children when they are afflicted. He "comes to our side" in our trials and upholds us under the weight of suffering.

AFFLICTION - 2Corinthians 1:4 (Descriptive word)
General usage: This word is used more in 2Corinthians than in any other N.T. book (1:4,6,8;2:4; 4:8,17;7:4,5;8:2,13). The Greek word is _thlipsis_, derived from the verb _thlibo_ (to press or afflict). The noun _thlipsis_ is translated "tribulation" or "affliction" most usually, but also has the ideas of "anguish," "trouble" and "persecution" in some passages.

The word thlipsis refers to sufferings due to the pressure of circumstances or the antagonism of persons. When this word is applied to believers, it almost always refers to pressures that come from external causes, rather than those that spring from inner turmoil.

Usage in context: The word refers to some specific pressures that came upon Paul when he was in Asia (note 2Cor.1:8,9); the cause is unclear. As a result of these severe afflictions, Paul despaired of life and was very close to death.

WEAKNESS - Romans 15:1-3 (Descriptive word)
General usage: This word occurs often in the N.T. The Greek word is *astheneia*, derived from *stheno* (strength). Asthenia means "without strength," "weak," "frail," "infirm." It is used of many different kinds of weakness: the weakness of the human body, the weakness of the law as a system, the weakness of Jesus in dying on the cross, the weakness of our spirit to prevail in prayer, and of general spiritual weakness or immaturity.

Usage in context: In Romans 15:1 astheneia refers to spiritual weakness and immaturity. The previous chapter of Romans deals with those who are "weak in faith." These are people who have not realized their freedom in Christ; they are still bound by old religious scruples such as refraining from certain foods. The weak in faith stand in contrast to those who have faith to eat all things, those whose spiritual maturity is sufficiently developed so that they are not bound by old regulations.

EDIFICATION - Romans 15:2 (Descriptive word)
General usage: The Greek word for "edification" is *oikodome* from *oikos* (house) and *demo* (to build). The idea is that of physically "building a house," and this is precisely the meaning the word has in many places. But the word oikodome was also used in a spiritual sense of "building the house of God." In fact, the people of God (the Church) are referred to with this same word (I Cor.3:9; Eph.2:21). The word is used of "spiritual upbuilding" in several key passages (Acts 20:32;

Eph.4:12,16,29; I Thess.5:11). Believers are to build up one another in their faith.

Usage in context: In Rom.15:2 the word has the idea of spiritual upbuilding. It is also found with this same meaning in the previous chapter (Rom.14:19). The opposite of "building up one another" is found in 14:20; "Do not tear down the work of God for the sake of food." The believer is likened to a work of God, something that He has been building for Himself. We are to contribute to God's building activity in the lives of fellow believers. We are not to hinder the work of God by our offensive actions.

PERFUME - Matthew 26:6-13 (Topical word)
Perfumes were commonly used in Biblical times for both religious and sanitary purposes. Special perfumes would be used when an important guest visited a home. Also, perfumes were used to prepare bodies for burial, both the body and the cloth wrapping coated with ointments. The kind of perfume used by the woman was "pure nard" (Mark 14:3), otherwise known as "spikenard ointment" (John 12:3). This perfume was very costly because it had to be imported from India in special, sealed containers. These sealed containers would only be broken on very special occasions, such as when the woman anointed Jesus in Matt. 26. It is apparent, therefore, that this woman was making a very special sacrifice of substantial value in pouring this perfume on Jesus.

BITHYNIA - Acts 16:6-10 (Topical word)
Bithynia was the northwest province of Asia Minor - a very mountainous and fertile region with heavy forests. The Romans conquered this area in 75 B.C. They had great interest in this region due to its strategic significance with good harbors and roads. It is unclear how the Christian church was established in Bithynia, since Paul was prevented from going into this region on his second journey.

Some scholars think that Peter was ministering in this area at about the same time. By the time Peter wrote his first letter, there were Christians scattered throughout Bithynia (I Pt.1:1). By the end of the first century there was a large population of Christians in this region. This is seen in letters from Pliny (110 A.D.) to the Roman Emperor Trajan where it is stated that the presence of so many Christians in the region had become an embarrassment to the Roman Empire!

GODS (of Moab) - Ruth 1:15-18 (Topical word)
The national deity of Moab was Chemosh. This god is mentioned in several places in the O.T. (Num.21:29; Jud.11:24; I Kg.11:7, 33; II Kg. 23:13; Jer.48:7,13,46). The Moabites honored Chemosh with such cruel rites as the sacrifice of infants in fire. These "people of Chemosh" seem to have been quite dedicated to their god (Num.21:29). They had priests and princes dedicated to serving Chemosh. Solomon made Israel sin by building a high place for Chemosh in Jerusalem. This high place remained for many years until King Josiah finally tore it down during his religious reforms in Israel. This was the god to whom Orpah returned, and to whom Ruth refused to return. Ruth chose Yahweh and His people over Chemosh and Moab.

7

From The Mind To The Feet

$\dagger$

But prove yourselves doers of the word, and not merely hearers who delude themselves. For if anyone is a hearer of the word and not a doer, he is like a man who looks at his natural face in a mirror; for once he has looked at himself and gone away, he has immediately forgotten what kind of person he was. But one who looks intently at the perfect law, the law of liberty, and abides by it, not having become a forgetful hearer but an effectual doer, this man shall be blessed in what he does (James 1:22-25).

Let's go back to the beginning of our discussion for a moment. At the outset of this book I argued that the synthetic method of Bible study - reading a book of the Bible over and over again - would fill your mind with the message of the text in a way that would be life changing. I made the case that when one's mind becomes saturated with the message of a book, the effect of this renewed mind will naturally begin to be seen and felt in one's daily life. In short, I was suggesting that in the synthetic method of study, there would be a natural flow from the mind to the feet; the *application* of Scripture would become an ongoing process, much like a program that is running quietly in the background of the computer of your mind.

There is, to be sure, a natural, free-flowing kind of application of Scripture that results from the synthetic method. The Scripture so deeply imbedded in your mind naturally oozes its way out into the daily footsteps of your life. I would refer to this as *unintentional* or *way-of-life* application resulting from a mind saturated with God's thoughts.

I would like to discuss, at this point, a further *intentional* step in the study process, namely, the analysis of Scripture for specific, life-related application points. Here, you are going back over the text to draw out lessons for yourself and others. Instead of waiting for the Holy Spirit to bring something to your mind, you are actually hunting for potential principles and applications that the passage conveys.

PRINCIPLES: DRAWING OUT THE TIMELESS TRUTHS

The first step in moving toward intentional personal application is drawing the *principles* out of a paragraph of Scripture. A principle is a timeless or universal statement of truth.

The various books of the Bible were written in definite time periods, to limited audiences. These books address issues and concerns that were relevant to the audiences in their day. Now we live in a different time, a different place. We face unique and varied situations of our own. One passage from Romans, therefore, must speak not only to the ancient inhabitants of Rome in their situation, but also to the modern readers in their situations. How can one passage, written to a specific audience in ancient times, have something to say to everyone, everywhere, in any age?

> *The practice of drawing out principles enables us to build bridges of relevance from the ancient Biblical text to the modern world in which we live.*

The practice of drawing out principles enables us to build bridges of relevance from the ancient Biblical text to the modern world in which we live. Principles are timeless truths; they are valid for every generation. Principles are universal truths; they are valid in every place where people live. Principles are the key to understanding how the Bible speaks to our situation today.

You have a paragraph analysis sitting in front of you. You have done several word studies and have grasped the meaning of the message in the paragraph. In other words, you know what the original author was saying to the original audience. Now, it is time to put your *principle eyeglasses* on. Look back over the passage. Meditate on the thoughts that it contains. Ask yourself: What are the timeless truths contained here? What are the principles valid for anyone and everyone? What are the fundamental lessons that this passage teaches?

Scan each verse thoughtfully and prayerfully. This is the point in Bible study where the Holy Spirit's ministry of *illumination* becomes especially powerful and personal. The Spirit is not simply interested in clarifying the *meaning* of the Biblical message; rather, He is deeply concerned that we grasp its *significance* for our lives today. Anyone can read the story of Jesus' crucifixion and understand intellectually what a Roman cross was, what it was made of, how it was used to execute people, and so on. But only under the Holy Spirit's personal illumination can a human heart grasp the incredible significance and life changing value of the cross of Jesus Christ. The Spirit really moves in to work with us as we scour the text for application and significance.

Write down the principles that you see in a given paragraph. You may have to refine and edit your principle statements so that they are concise and accurate. Writing good principle statements is an art, but it comes easy to most who work at it. You can exercise your creativity here in developing an especially memorable principle statement. A well-edited principle statement makes an excellent teaching tool as you seek to communicate God's truth to others.

Following are some sample principle statements, including the text from which they were drawn. At the end of this chapter there are more samples.

> The measure of our forgiveness for others should reflect the measure of God's forgiveness for us (Matthew 18:21-35).

> We should honor those whom God has placed in authority, even when they seem unworthy of such honor (1Samuel 24:6).

> Humility of mind personally fosters unity in the body of Christ corporately (Philippians 2:1-11).

Notice several things about these principle statements: First, they are concise. Ideally, you should be able to state a principle in 20 words or less. Second, they are accurate. They are based upon a proper understanding of the meaning of the passage. A principle statement is only as good as the study that supports it! Principles must be true to the text. Third, they are stated in a general way so that anyone who hears them can relate to them. They are not restricted to a time or to an audience. They are universal, timeless truths.

APPLICATIONS: ISOLATING THE SPECIFIC ACTION POINTS

Principle statements are intended to be general so that anyone, anywhere can apply them. Application statements, on the other hand, are to be specific, selective and very personal, so that *you* or *those to whom you are speaking* can apply them. Here we allow God's truth to touch our personal lives; we allow His Word to move right in and rearrange our values, our priorities, our schedules, our attitudes, our actions, our relationships, etc.

I was talking with a friend, recently, who was preparing to go on a church mission trip. This was a step of faith for her and involved overcoming a certain amount of fear. She explained that she had been reading in the book of Joshua and came across God's instructions to Joshua:

Have I not commanded you? Be strong and courageous! Do not tremble or be dismayed, for the Lord your God is with you wherever you go (Joshua 1:9).

This woman saw a general principle in this verse, namely, that we need not walk in fear when we are walking in obedience to God, even if the journey ahead seems difficult. If God has commanded us to go, then we can be strong and courageous as we walk with Him on a difficult journey.

She then made a specific application of this principle to her own life with regard to the decision to join the mission trip. She made a personal commitment to give her fear over to God and to join the team.

This is a perfect example of: 1) Seeing the meaning of a passage for the original audience, 2) Seeing the principle, or, timeless truth for all ages, and 3) making a specific personal application to one's own life. That is allowing God's Word to change our lives today in very tangible ways. That is getting the Bible from the mind to the feet. That is, most commonly, how the Holy Spirit *speaks to us* today.

As with principle statements, it is a good idea to get in the habit of writing out your application statements. Perhaps you can write these in your personal diary, or your prayer journal. A good application statement should be personal. It should contain the words, "I will. . ." and specify the action to be taken. By stating the application in this way, you are essentially making a commitment to do something about God's truth.

Further, good applications are selective. You cannot possibly apply all of the principles that you draw from one paragraph. Select the one most striking principle from a paragraph and really work at acting upon it. As you look over your list of principles, you should ask yourself: Which of these principles touches upon a real area of need in my life? Which of these do I need to work out?

A good application should be *specific*. Don't beat around the bush when writing application statements. "I will be more forgiving," is not specific enough. Get to the point.   Following are application statements that might grow out of the principle statements cited above.

Principle: The measure of our forgiveness for others should reflect the measure of God's forgiveness for us (Matthew 18:21-35).
Application: Because of how freely God has forgiven me for my own sins, I will forgive Bill for his actions toward me. I will not take into account this wrong suffered. I will forgive this debt.

Principle: We should honor those whom God has placed in authority, even when they seem unworthy of such honor (1Samuel 24:6).
Application: I will show respect for my local district official and treat him with honor, even though I find myself at odds with him over certain values and policy issues for our community. I will not lift my hand against this individual or speak evil of him. I will, instead, pray for him to become a man who honors God with his life.

Principle: Humility of mind personally fosters unity in the body of Christ corporately (Philippians 2:1-11).
Application: I will express to Tom how much I appreciate his ministry in our church, and I will ask him if there is anything I can do to support him in his work. Whenever I catch myself comparing my work to his, I will pray for him to have success for God's glory.

At the end of this chapter you will find more samples of principles and applications. I close this chapter with a familiar story that Jesus told concerning the importance of putting the Word into action.

TWO KINDS OF BIBLE STUDENTS
At the end of the Sermon on the Mount (Matthew 5-7), Jesus painted a very vivid picture of two kinds of people. Jesus was not interested in promoting mere head-knowledge. He wanted to see lives changed as a result of His words.   This illustration served to emphasize the priority of acting upon the Word of God, rather than hearing and neglecting the message.

Therefore everyone who hears these words of Mine, and acts upon them, may be compared to a wise man, who built his house upon the rock. And the rain descended, and the floods came, and the winds blew, and burst against that house; and yet it did not fall, for it had been founded upon the rock. And everyone who hears these words of Mine, and does not act upon them, will be like a foolish man, who built his house upon the sand. And the rain descended, and the floods came, and the winds blew, and burst against that house; and it fell, and great was its fall (Matthew 7:24-27).

Both men were *building houses*, meaning that both were hearing the words of Jesus, and building a certain type of spiritual life as a result. Further, both men *encountered violent storms* which tested the relative value of their houses. These storms picture the trials of life which assault each of us, challenging the very credibility of our spiritual lives. The storms show what we are really made of.

Building and encountering storms...is where the similarity between these two men ends. The wise man dug right down to the rock before beginning to build; the foolish man hurriedly began constructing his

In this parable, the rock upon which the wise man built represents hearing and doing Jesus' words. The sand, on the other hand, represents hearing and neglecting Jesus' words.

house upon the sand. When the storms came, the wise man's house stood firm, while the foolish man's house fell flat. Concerning the house that fell, Jesus adds, "and *great* was its fall!"

In this parable, the rock upon which the wise man built represents *hearing and doing Jesus' words*. The sand, on the other hand, represents *hearing and neglecting Jesus' words*. The wise man heard and applied God's message. The Word went from his head to his feet. The foolish man, in contrast, heard but did not apply the same message from God. The rock illustrates obedient application, while the sand shows lackadaisical carelessness. This little parable is a big warning against failure to apply God's Word to our lives.

God is still speaking today. His words are just as much alive when we read them in the Bible, as they were when He delivered them in person. People are still listening to God's Word today. We read His words, we hear Him speak, and those who listen to God's voice today are still falling into two basic categories.

There are those who work at applying God's Word to their personal lives. These are wise people who are building solid spiritual lives. Then, there are those who are not working at application. They read, they study, they grow in knowledge, but they do not apply and obey. By their negligence in the area of personal application, they are setting themselves up for calamity. Stability or calamity - the outcome depends upon moving the Word from your mind to your feet.

OVERVIEW OF THE BIBLE STUDY PROCESS

THE SYNTHETIC PHASE OF BIBLE STUDY

REPEATED READINGS   Gaining a synthetic, overall impression of the book. Filling the mind with the actual words of Scripture. Forming a mental blueprint of the book.

↓

BACKGROUND STUDY   Enhancing the reading phase by getting knee-deep into the historical setting: author, recipient, setting, purpose. Becoming thoroughly familiar with the life and times of the book.

↓

THEME STATEMENT   A capsule statement of the book's central message based on your own repeated readings. This is the heart of the book in just one, simple sentence, perhaps linked to a key verse in the book itself.

↓

SYNTHETIC OUTLINE   An overview of the general movement of the book from beginning to end, showing how the theme is develop in major sections.

THE ANALYTICAL PHASE OF BIBLE STUDY

ANALYTICAL OUTLINE   A paragraph-by-paragraph road map of the book which serves as a guide for your ongoing analysis.

↓

PARAGRAPH ANALYSIS Paragraph display helps you analyze a discourse paragraph; paragraph overview helps you analyze a narrative paragraph.

↓

WORD STUDIES Topical word studies or descriptive word studies; words selected based on potential to help you grasp the author's message.

↓

PRINCIPLES & Timeless truths stated simply, accompanied
APPLICATIONS by specific, personal application points relevant to your life and those whom you teach.

SAMPLE PRINCIPLES & APPLICATIONS

PRACTICAL ANALYSIS - 2nd Corinthians 1:3-5

Principles
1. The God of all comfort will come to our aid in every affliction.
2. Experiencing God's comfort in our affliction equips us to comfort others.
3. Though Christians will surely suffer, we know that God's comfort will always be sufficient.

Application
I will thank God, by faith, for the suffering that I am experiencing. I will do this because I know that He is equipping me to serve Him more effectively in the future in comforting others who are hurting in similar ways.

PRACTICAL ANALYSIS - Joshua 24:14-15

Principles

1. God's past acts of faithfulness should motivate us to serve Him wholeheartedly.
2. The question is not whether we will serve a god, but which god will we serve.

Application

I will start a notebook in which I record God's acts of faithfulness in my life. I will begin by recalling His faithfulness in the past and I will keep this notebook current. In this way I will be motivated to serve God with my whole heart, as I see how faithful He has been to me.

PRACTICAL ANALYSIS - Romans 15:1-3

Principles

1. Strong Christians are obligated to bear the weakness of less mature Christians.
2. No Christian should be driven by the motivation of self-pleasure.
3. We should always seek to build up, rather than tear down the people around us.

Application

I will seek to build up Jim by not criticizing him and by encouraging him in his good points. I will make a list of his good points and really make the effort to let him know that I appreciate these things in his life.

PRACTICAL ANALYSIS - RUTH 1:15-18

<u>Principles</u>
1. True loyalty involves more than lip service; it calls for total, unreserved commitment.
2. Convictions are those beliefs from which we cannot be swayed, regardless of the pressure.

<u>Application</u>
I will try to develop my convictions with regard to personal evangelism. I have been unconvinced for years of my need to share my faith, and peer pressure has caused me to be silent. I will allow God to deepen my convictions in this area by attending the evangelism class that the church is offering over the next two months.

8

The Rules Of The Read

$\dagger$

I thank God for the man who taught me to read and study the Bible *for myself.* What a privilege it is to be able to open the Bible, dig into the tools, think over the meaning, and form my own conclusions. Personal Bible study leads to personal convictions. I spent too many years letting someone else decide for me what the Bible says. I believe that we need to spend more of our time abiding in the Word ourselves, drinking personally from the well of Scripture.

With privilege, however, there always comes a corresponding responsibility. If you want to drive a car, you must learn the rules of the road. If you want to practice law, you must learn the rules of the courtroom. If you want to develop property, you must learn the rules of the planning commission. If you want to interpret the Bible for yourself, you must learn the rules of the read.

The privilege of personal Bible study comes hand in hand with the responsibility to read and study with accuracy. Paul said to Timothy: **Be diligent to present yourself approved to God as a workman who does not need to be ashamed, handling accurately the word of truth (2Timothy 2:15).**

That means, quite simply, that there is an accurate as well as an inaccurate way to handle Scripture. Or, to put it differently, every method of reading and interpreting the Bible is not equally valid. Validity in interpretation depends upon our adherence to the rules of the read.   Technically speaking, we are talking here about *hermeneutics*, or, the science of interpretation.   Interpreting the Bible is not a subjective art form; it is a discipline with clear guidelines.

The idea of *reading by the rules* applies across the board, regardless of the intellectual level at which you are studying Scripture. I have taught hermeneutics to village folks in Asia and Africa, and I have taught these same principles to highly educated Americans. You do not need advanced degrees to be a sound interpreter of Scripture. From early ages, my own four children learned to grapple with the various sections of the Bible and to come up with sound interpretations.   On the other hand, I have seen some extremely brilliant, highly educated individuals approach the Bible in violation of the rules of the read, resulting in confusing and fanciful suggestions as to what the Bible means. The rules of the read are easy to understand. All serious students of sacred Scripture should become familiar with them.

THE PLACE OF INTERPRETATION IN THE DIVINE COMMUNICATION PROCESS

The importance of the rules of the read may be seen when we consider the place of interpretation in the overall communication process between God and man. Think of God as the communicator and yourself as the receiver. God has a message in His mind that He wants to get clearly into your mind.   How will God accomplish the communication of this message? He has chosen four basic steps in order to get His message into your mind, without distortion.

Inspiration: Step one, inspiration, involves the production of the original documents. The Holy Spirit led the original writers as they produced their writings. The result of His supernatural leading was that these human authors wrote the "Word of God" (2Timothy 3:16; 2Peter 1:20,21). The Biblical documents bear the handprint of God on them. This is inspiration then, the process whereby God produced the written documents through human authors. Inspiration is a completed work. We have a full revelation from God in the 66 inspired books of the Bible.

Transmission: The second step in the divine communication process, transmission, involves the movement of God's message from one person to the next. If inspiration is a vertical process (from God down to man) then transmission is a horizontal process (from man to man). Transmission happens in several ways:

Early in the history of God's Word, transmission was accomplished largely by word of mouth. One individual would memorize a portion of Scripture and then recite it to others who would also memorize it. This explains why there are so many mnemonic devices (memory aids) buried within the pages of Scripture. These devices helped people recall the text so that they could recite it accurately.

Eventually, the task of transmission fell to the scribes in ancient Israel, who devoted their lives to the reproduction of accurate copies of the Scriptures. Sitting in groups, with a reader in front of them, the scribes would meticulously copy each letter of the text, comparing their results with one another to insure total accuracy of the copies. They were fanatical about flawless transmission of the sacred text.

Today, transmission is carried out by the printing press, as copies of the Word of God are printed and distributed to the general public in rapid fashion and high volume. Walk into a bookstore, purchase a Bible, and transmission has taken place! The Word of God is in your hands when you walk out the door.

Again, note that this step is done for you. You do not need to listen to and memorize Scripture to get it, nor do you have to become a scribe and make yourself a copy. If you have a Bible in your possession, then transmission has already taken place. The message is in your hands, inspired and transmitted.

Translation: The third step in the divine communication process is translation. The task of the translator is to transfer the Biblical message from one set of linguistic symbols to another so that it is readable by those who do not read ancient Hebrew and Greek. The great difficulty in translation arises in thoroughly mastering the original languages in which the Bible was written. Fortunately, many men and women devote their lives to the mastery of biblical languages and the translation of the texts.

Scholars working in committees develop the typical modern translation. Not only are they careful to follow the most accurate manuscript evidence for every passage, but they also work diligently to select modern language equivalents of ancient words and phrases so that the precise meaning will be accurately conveyed to the reader. Comparing and crosschecking one another's work, these translation teams provide us with accurate, up-to-date translations in our own modern languages.

Again, this work is done for you. If you hold a Bible in your hands that has been translated into your own native language, you can thank the scholars who spent thousands of hours poring over every word! Modern 'scribes' they are, these men and women who give us the words of God in our own languages.

Three steps - inspiration, transmission and translation - have been done for you. The Bible has been divinely inspired, faithfully transmitted, and carefully translated. The Word of God sits in front of you as an open book, and only one step remains in order for God to get His message clearly into your mind. Now, perhaps you can better understand the importance of . . .

Interpretation: The fourth and final step in the divine communication process is interpretation. The student of Scripture sits with the book open before him and seeks to understand the meaning

of the original author.   Although the first three steps have been
faithfully performed for you, the entire communication process can be
thwarted if you are not careful in the crucial step of interpretation.
We must exercise care at this point.   There is no room for haphazard
or subjective hermeneutics.   The goal of interpretation is to grasp
what the original author meant, without distortion.   The means to this
goal is simply to follow a sound set of hermeneutical guidelines, *the
rules of the read.*

THE PROCESS OF WORD COMMUNICATION
from the mind of God to the mind of man

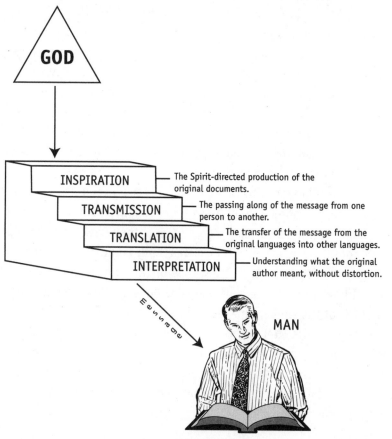

In this chapter we will survey seven key principles of interpretation. These are not my rules, nor are they rules that are unique to the study of the Bible. These are widely accepted guidelines for reading literature in general. These same rules would be understood and applied by people reading a newspaper, a mystery novel, a legal document or the book of Romans. In most cases, people read with these rules operating in the background of their understanding, applying these rules almost without thinking about them.

SEVEN KEY RULES OF THE READ
Reading Rule #1: PRIORITIZE THE LITERAL MEANING

Usually, when people speak or write they intend to be understood literally. Obviously, communicators will use figures of speech here and there, but for the most part the typical communicator assumes that the audience will take the message at face value. It does not matter whether you are reading Romans, listening to the evening news, or reading a fishing magazine; the basis of most communication is a literal understanding of words and phrases. There is really no other starting point for communication.

With the Bible, as with other literature, the 'literal principle,' is the first and foundational rule of all serious reading and interpretation. *If the plain, literal sense makes good sense, then seek no other sense!* Much confusion regarding Biblical teaching could have been avoided throughout history by the observance of this fundamental rule of the read. I have not taken a count on this, but I would estimate that well over 90% of the words, phrases and sentences of the Bible were meant to be taken quite literally. There are portions of Scripture that have a higher percentage of figurative language, particularly the poetic and prophetic sections, but even these parts of Scripture are heavy in literal material. The non-literal material is always couched within the bigger literal framework.

The literal principle warns against *reading into* a passage a meaning that was never intended by the original author (allegorizing or spiritualizing a text by finding hidden meanings). Nor are we to *read around* the literal meaning in order to escape difficult teachings or ideas (labeling texts as mythology or legend when they do not seem to fit our rational mindset). We are to let the Bible speak for itself by giving priority to a literal understanding of its words. Simply put: God meant just what He said!

I could give multiple examples of the violation of the literal principle, but let me mention just one glaring violation that is common, current and very dangerous.

Modern attempts to rediscover the "historical Jesus" by *demythologizing* the gospel accounts provide a good example of violation of the literal principle. In trying to determine who the historical Jesus was, the attempt is made to discard the literal understanding of most of the gospel records, to strip away the "myths" of the gospel accounts. Anything that sounds supernatural is generally considered a myth (e.g. the virgin birth, the resurrection, the miracles of Jesus, etc.). Concerning this practice of demythologizing the New Testament, Robert Traina explains:

Frequently in order to remove that which cannot be comprehended or accepted by the reason, one will declare that certain events are myths rather than actual historical occurrences. They are therefore like the shell of a walnut which may be discarded as soon as the spiritual truth it conveys, which is the nutmeat, is discovered.[1]

Quite simply, this is a violation of the literal principle in the name of modern rationalism. Since a miracle is, by very definition, supernatural, it is not natural or rational and must, therefore, be rejected as a literal, factual record. Therefore, since the purported miracle did not *literally* happen, the author must be telling us a myth, fable, parable or some other figurative story that has a hidden meaning. Out goes the literal principle and in walks the subjective-guess principle. The story means whatever you want it to mean!

For example, I have heard interpreters of the Bible argue that the "miracle" of the feeding of the 5,000 was not really a miracle at all. It has been suggested that Jesus was standing at the mouth of a cave and the disciples were handing him bread and fish from inside the cave as He was giving it out to the multitudes. It only looked like a miracle to the crowd of witnesses. (Although, the fact that Jesus and the disciples had so much bread and fish hidden in that particular cave would be a minor miracle in itself!) Or, a more dignified version of this non-literal approach goes like this: When the little boy opened up his lunch basket and gave up the five loaves and the few small fish, the crowd was overwhelmed by his kindness and unselfishness. The result was that all of the people opened up their lunch packets, which they had been selfishly hiding under their robes, and began to generously share with one another. In other words, this was a "miracle of sharing" and we should all be similarly generous.

Nonsense! Any careful student of the gospels can see that the primary significance of this miracle is the powerful statement which it makes concerning the *person of Christ*. The feeding of the 5,000 is there to show the reader, in a rather climactic way, that Jesus was the Son of God, not that He was shrewd, or that people were generous.

The student of Scripture must seize the importance of the literal principle at the very outset. Interpretive chaos reigns when we do not give priority to a literal understanding of the words and phrases of the Bible. All serious interpretation starts with the literal principle. Any other starting point ends in utter confusion and personal subjectivity.

We will discuss the presence of figurative language in the Bible as one of our seven rules of the read. There is a responsible way to deal with non-literal language. We must recognize, however, that if we do not *start with* the literal principle, then all objective dealing with the message of the Bible evaporates into thin air.   The reality is that for the most part, the Bible *means exactly what it says!*

Reading Rule #2: CONTEXT IS KING

Take a football and put it on the bag at second base in a baseball park.   Then, ask an observer what the football means.   It means nothing because the football has been ripped away from its natural context.   Now put the football on the 30-yard line in a football stadium and suddenly it takes on its proper contextual meaning.   One of the teams is on the 30-yard line and is driving down the field. Things have meaning in their natural context.   Taken out of context things either have a wrong meaning or no meaning at all.

"Context" is defined by Webster as, "the parts of a discourse that surround a word or passage and can throw light on its meaning."[2]   The interpreter must pay careful attention to the context of a passage as a primary factor in determining the meaning.   To put it simply: Context is king!

The rule of context, like the literal principle, is very often violated with dangerous results. As James Sire notes in his book *Scripture Twisting*, the cults are famous for the violation of the context principle.

From the standpoint of the Bible as literature, the simplest error of reading is the failure to consider the immediate context of the verse or passage in question. The literature of the cults is filled with illustrations of this basic mistake.[3]

There are various levels of context for a Biblical passage.   The *immediate context* is the paragraph in which a passage is found.   The *near context* is the entire book in which the passage is situated.   The *wider context* would consist of other books of the Bible which are related to the book in which the passage is found.

Always begin your search for interpretive clues in the immediate context and work outwards to the wider context.   Look for close-at-hand clues such as explanatory phrases, contrasts or comparisons, definitions, illustrations, etc., that will give you the proper interpretation of the word or phrase. If the immediate context leaves you uncertain, search the entire book for similar phrases that might shed light on the question. Still wider in the search, this same author may have used similar wording in another of his writings, or another author writing the same kind of material might have used similar ideas.

Here again, we see the value of synthetic readings. Reading and re-reading a book saturates you with context. You have a good picture of the overall message, which increases the likelihood that in your mind you will cross-reference a word or phrase naturally. Also, this rule of context proves the value of paragraph analysis. In paragraph analysis I suggested that you first consider the message of the whole paragraph, before you tear apart individual words and phrases. Again, this is a process of setting individual sentences in the field of context. And with word studies I taught you to assign meaning to an individual word only after considering carefully its immediate context. The rule of context is pervasive in the Bible study process.

Let me give you a brief illustration of the context principle at work. I was reading Psalm 34 recently. Verse 10 reads:

The young lions do lack and suffer hunger; but they who seek the Lord shall not be in want of any good thing (Psalm 34:10).

Taken out of context this verse could be understood as a blanket promise of blessing along these lines: *If I seek the Lord, He will give me good things. I will not be in want, I will never be hungry, I will not suffer bad things or experience pain, difficulty or loss. The lions may hurt, but I won't, because I seek the Lord.*

Yet, set in the immediate context of the 34th Psalm, this verse cannot be taken as a blanket of blessing. It really teaches something entirely different, something much more profound. Look at verse 18:

The Lord is near to the brokenhearted, and saves those who are crushed in spirit (Psalm 34:18).

Read on to the next verse, which is rather striking:
Many are the afflictions of the righteous, but the Lord delivers him out of them all (Psalm 34:19).

Many are the afflictions *of the righteous!* I recall the first time I really studied this Psalm. When I came to this verse, I thought I had encountered a misprint. Don't afflictions belong with the bad guys, and blessings with the good guys? Yet, this Psalm shows that afflictions will certainly come upon the godly person. The 34th Psalm is actually a song of thanksgiving for God's faithfulness during a time of peril and difficulty for King David. Far from promising absolute prosperity and exemption from difficulty, this song promises that difficulties will come, but that God can be trusted amidst the difficulties when we cry out to Him to be our deliverer. He will come to our aid and vindicate our confidence in Him in the face of critics and enemies who would challenge us and question our faith in God. Set in the wider context of the many other "Psalms of lament and complaint" the 34th Psalm is promising God's provision, power and companionship *in the midst of the certain afflictions* that will come upon the righteous.

> *Context is king in the interpretation of words, phrases and verses in the Bible. Sound theology grows as we wrestle with passages of Scripture in context.*

This is simply one example of how the context principle works. Yet, you can see how theology and practice hinge upon understanding things in context. The surrounding words and phrases help us to properly understand the meaning of other words and phrases. Context is king in the interpretation of words, phrases and verses in the Bible. Sound theology grows as we wrestle with passages of Scripture in context. Never accept as truth a doctrine that is built upon a Scripture isolated from its context.

Reading Rule #3: LET SCRIPTURE INTERPRET SCRIPTURE

The third rule of the read extends the context principle to the 66 books of the Bible as a whole. The Bible is its own best commentary. No other book or person can provide a more authoritative comment on the Bible than the comments the Bible makes on itself. By comparing one Scripture with another, therefore, the interpreter can secure an infallible opinion on a difficult passage.

This interpretive principle grows out of our basic view of the Bible as an *inspired* book. Because the Holy Spirit is the unifying author of the Bible, all 66 books have an underlying unity, consistency and coherence. Though many different human writers penned the various books over a period of some 1,500 years, the Holy Spirit guided them to produce books that present a story and a message that fits together.

Therefore, what the Spirit of God revealed through one author in one time period may prove helpful in understanding what He revealed to another author in another situation. It is interesting, for example, to see how the interpretation of a single prophetic book is aided by an understanding of the prophetic literature as a whole. Similarly, the four gospels shed light on one another. The 13 letters of Paul often interpret one another. The book of James has many contact points with Jesus' Sermon on the Mount (Matthew 5-7). The Olivet Discourse (Matthew 24, Mark 13) has close ties with Daniel, Revelation, and the Thessalonian letters.

Here is an example from church history that shows the value of this principle. It is well known that Martin Luther had difficulty with the book of James. Because of his emphasis on salvation by grace through faith, as taught in books like Romans and Galatians, the

Protestant reformer dismissed the book of James as a "right strawy epistle" and relegated it to a secondary position at the back of his Bible.

Yet, time and consideration has shown the incredible value of books like James, 2Peter, 1John and Hebrews, all of which place a significant emphasis on the fruit of salvation (i.e., a changed life).   In other words, true saving faith (Romans, Galatians) produces a changed life (James).   Sanctification grows out of justification and cannot safely be separated from it. Paul, reacting to the dangerous Jewish legalism of his day, was arguing in both Romans and Galatians that salvation cannot be attained by the works of the law.   Luther seized upon the relevance of this message based on the works-oriented situation in his own day.   Yet, James, perhaps reacting to some

Let the 66 books make their case in full. They are a unit, and they must be understood in light of one another.

who had turned God's grace into a license for sin, was showing that saving faith is accompanied by a changed life. Faith is the root; works are the fruit.   Paul and James interpret one another, providing a beautifully whole picture. Scripture is coherent.

Let Scripture interpret Scripture.   The Bible is its own best commentary!   You will notice that over time, as you study increasing numbers of books of the Bible, you will form in your mind a kind of *theological system* that helps you to interpret Scripture. The theology of individual books begins to add up in your mind, forming a theology of the Bible as a whole. This holistic Biblical theology, in turn, serves as an excellent tool in the interpreting of individual passages. Let the 66 books make their case in full. They are a unit, and they must be understood in light of one another.

Reading Rule #4: THE ORIGINAL SETTING IS THE CANVAS

When the President of the United States speaks, he does so in different settings. His words must be understood in light of the specific settings in which he speaks. For example, a State of the Union address is one kind of message. A talk with an elementary school class is a different kind of message. A speech given in a friendly foreign country is another kind of message; one given in a not-so-friendly foreign country is yet another message. A casual, off-the-record comment made while flying on Air Force One, is yet a different message. What makes these messages distinct is the various settings in which they are delivered. To be fair to the President, an interpreter reading a manuscript of any one of these message would have to be familiar with the setting in which the message was delivered; otherwise, he might misunderstand the emphasis which the President was making and impute a meaning never intended.

Every book of the Bible was written in the context of a historical setting. The meaning of a message is intrinsically linked to that original setting. It is important, therefore, to interpret a section of Biblical literature in light of the original setting. In other words, we must put ourselves in the situation of the original recipients as much as possible when seeking to understand the meaning of their correspondence.

As Terry says:

It is of the first importance . . . to ascertain who the author was, and to determine the time, the place, and the circumstances of his writing. The interpreter should, therefore, endeavor to take himself from the present, and to transport himself into the historical position of his author, look through his eyes, note his surroundings, feel with his heart, and catch his emotion.[4]

Traina, speaking of this same hermeneutical principle, calls it the process of "re-creation."

Thus the process of re-creation involves such a complete identification of the interpreter with the authors of the Bible that he relives the experiences which were entailed in its writing. It means recapturing the attitudes, motives, thoughts, and emotions of its writers and of those concerning whom they wrote.[5]

Once again, the value of previously mentioned procedures is clear. The background analysis that you performed near the beginning of the Bible study process is designed to familiarize you with the historical and cultural setting of the book. The better your background study, the better footing you will be on when it comes to interpreting the author's message.

The historical books of both the Old and New Testaments often provide valuable historical background material for the study of other books. You will also profit much from the research of scholars on the historical and cultural background of the Bible. For example, Alfred Edersheim's classic work, *The Life and Times of Jesus the Messiah*[6] contains a wealth of detailed background material which is useful in the study of the gospels. The *IVP Bible Background Commentary* by Craig Keener[7] is another good example of a scholarly work that puts in your hands relevant background information to aid in the interpretation process. There are many works of this sort now available, and they are excellent in deepening our understanding of the world of the Bible, both Old and New Testaments.

The importance of this interpretive rule is highlighted by a study of the book of 1st Corinthians. There, Paul addressed numerous practical issues growing out of the everyday life of early Christians in the cultural context of Corinth. Issues such as foods, dress codes, hairstyles, lawsuits, marriage and divorce, etc. are all addressed *against the backdrop of life in Corinth*. It is essential, therefore, when studying a book like 1st Corinthians, to learn all that you can about everyday life in that setting.

> *Meaning is attached to setting.*
> *The interpreter must reconstruct*
> *the setting of the original author*
> *and recipients and read the book*
> *in that light.*

The key idea here is simply this: Meaning is attached to setting. The interpreter must reconstruct the setting of the original author and recipients and read the book in that light. We must be cautious when we read the Bible in light of our contemporary setting. This is a valid practice in determining *relevance* and *application*, but it is an invalid practice when determining *meaning*. The meaning must be sought in terms of the historical and cultural background of the Bible itself. Then we can safely draw accurate principles that are relevant and applicable for our present day.

Reading Rule #5: TUNE IN TO THE AUDIENCE

Going a step beyond setting, the correct interpretation of any passage must come in light of the original recipients of the message. In other words, when you read a book of the Bible, you are reading someone else's mail. Louis Berkhof says:

For the correct understanding of a writing or discourse, it is of the utmost importance to know for whom it was first of all intended. This applies particularly to those books of the Bible that are of an occasional character, such as the prophetical books and the New Testament Epistles. These were naturally adapted to the special circumstances and the particular needs of the reader.[8]

In my library I have an old book that is a collection of letters written by the English pastor John Newton, author of the hymn *Amazing Grace*. These 158 letters were sent to 25 different friends, parishioners and coworkers during the course of Newton's ministry. The understanding of each letter requires some sense of who the 25 original recipients were.

For example, there are two letters addressed to a "Mr. A__ B__." (All of the recipients are anonymous.) It is evident from reading these two letters that Mr. A__ B__ was a man with whom Newton was having an ongoing debate over the Christian faith. Mr. A__ B__ was a card-playing, party-going Deist who scoffed at Newton's profound faith, referring to the Christians as "enthusiasts" (i.e., fanatics). The most striking thing about Mr. A__ B__ is that he had just recovered from a brush with death at the time of the first letter. Some mortal illness had taken hold of him and he had barely escaped with his life. Newton is anxious to know if this life-threatening experience has made any impact on him in terms of his openness to the truth about God. The first letter is, in essence, a warning from Newton not to allow such experiences to pass without serious reflection on one's views and improvement in one's life.

Interestingly, the second letter to Mr. A__ B__ reveals that he has become further hardened in his stance against Newton's faith in Christ. Apparently, he had responded to Newton's first letter indicating that the pass with death had virtually no impact on him, other than urging him on to further indulgences in the pleasures of life! Newton uses strong language to warn his friend that he is being shortsighted, not giving due consideration to the shallowness of his worldview. Newton has experienced *both* worldliness and godliness, while his friend has only experienced worldliness. Newton wished that his friend could taste the pleasures of godliness. He closes by warning his friend that if he does not take eternal issues seriously now, it will be too late and he will find himself standing in judgment: "Sooner or later, God will meet you!"

These two letters are quite unique among the 158 letters of Newton. He does not speak in this same way to the other 24 recipients of his letters. An understanding of Newton's message and meaning requires some appreciation for who the original recipient was. I am literally reading someone else's mail.

The same principle of interpretation applies to the 66 books of the Bible. Take, for example, Paul's letters to Timothy. A correct understanding of these letters begins with the identification of the original recipient as a relatively young man who was in a leadership position in a local church. Paul's admonitions concerning Timothy's conduct in the church must be understood in light of Timothy's age, gender and position.

When we read the Old Testament prophets, we must bear in mind that we are reading material that was originally addressed to Israel, a nation that was bound by a covenant with Yahweh. The prophets are acting as covenant enforcers, reminding Israel of the blessings and curses associated with the covenant.

The gospel of Matthew was addressed to a primarily Jewish audience, seeking to show them that Jesus was the long-awaited Messiah of Old Testament expectation. This helps to explain many of the unique features of his gospel. Galatians is a strong rebuke toward legalism written to a local church that had recently been infiltrated by false teachers. The Judaizers were teachers who strongly persuaded Gentile Christians that they must submit to the stipulations of Judaism, including circumcision and dietary regulations in order to be first-class Christians. An understanding of the background of the original audience will help you to see why Paul spoke in such strong terms in this correspondence.

> *Always recognize the original audience when seeking to determine the meaning of a text. When you study the Bible, you are reading someone else's mail.*

Always recognize the original audience when seeking to determine the meaning of a text. When you study the Bible, you are reading someone else's mail. Applications to your own life will only be reliable when they rest upon the foundation of a proper recognition of the original audience. The first question is: What did the message mean to them? The second question is: In light of this, what does it mean for me?

Reading Rule #6: WATCH FOR FIGURES OF SPEECH

The language of the Bible is the everyday language of the ancient world. As such, it has one thing in common with everyday language today: the use of figures of speech. Just as you might use a figure of speech to enhance your message, so the Biblical writers often found it appropriate to use them to make their message clearer.

The problem of interpreting figurative language in the Bible is illustrated by McQuilkin as follows;

All human languages are filled with talk that is not literal, but Eastern languages are especially full of figures of speech. Since these languages are foreign to us, that is all the more reason to work hard at understanding exactly what the author had in mind. There is the hurdle of distance in language and culture, and there is also the hurdle of figurative language. Consider the plight of a foreigner seeking to understand the English word 'hang.' A literal definition is easy to come by, but what is he to think when he hears, as a foreigner, that he has many hang-ups; that he should indeed hang loose and allow his true feelings to hang out? If he searches out those idioms carefully, he still may be at a loss to know why someone is absent because of a hangover, or when he is told, in spite of all the obstacles to understanding that he should not only hang on, but hang in there.[9]

It would be nearly impossible to give a hermeneutical rule book for dealing with all types of figurative language in the Bible. As Terry notes, such a system would be highly impractical.

It is scarcely necessary, and, indeed, quite impracticable, to lay down specific rules for determining when language is used figuratively and when literally. It is an old and oft repeated hermeneutical principle that words should be understood in their literal sense unless such literal

> *In other words, if the plain sense makes good sense, seek no other sense (literal principle), but if the plain sense makes nonsense, then you may be looking at a figure of speech (figurative principle).*

interpretation involves a manifest contradiction or absurdity. [10]

In other words, if the plain sense makes good sense, seek no other sense (literal principle), but if the plain sense makes nonsense, then you may be looking at a figure of speech (figurative principle). The recognition of figurative language is basically a matter of good, common sense.

When you suspect that figurative language is being used, seek to understand the figure in the normal, customary, cultural sense. It is very likely that the figure of speech will be somehow tied to everyday life in the setting of the book. You will, therefore, probably find yourself engaging in further background research to properly understand the life setting of figurative language. Commentaries, Bible dictionaries and encyclopedias will prove helpful here.

For example, if you were studying the parable of the ten virgins (Matt.25:1-13) you should try to understand the normal, cultural procedure by which a wedding procession took place, *not the way our modern weddings take place*. By studying the figure in its historical setting, the picture becomes clear as you see it from the same perspective that Jesus and His listeners saw it.

Often, figures of speech will be explained in the immediate context. Whenever a figure of speech is accompanied by an explanation, then we should rest our search for answers with the explanation provided in the text. Several of the parables of Jesus, for example, are accompanied by clear, simple explanations (e.g. the parable of the sower, Matt.13:1-23). In the Hebrew poetry of the Old Testament, one line will parallel or contrast the next line, thus rendering numerous figures of speech more comprehensible. Always scour the immediate context for clues as to the proper interpretation of figurative language. Usually, the clues are close at hand.

Put your thinking cap on when you encounter language in the Bible that sounds figurative. Failure to recognize figurative language can lead you into great error.

Not many years ago I read of a young man who took the following statement literally:

...and if your hand causes you to stumble, cut it off...and if your foot causes you to stumble, cut it off...and if your eye causes you to stumble, cast it out...(Mark 9:43-47)

The misguided young man followed these instructions to the letter and mutilated himself. Now stop and think for a moment: If you cut out one eye, will that prevent you from seeing the things that cause you to sin? Since all Christians still deal with temptation and sin, are we to reason that Jesus wanted all Christians to mutilate themselves? And what kind of an attractive witness would it be to the world if they saw that all Christians went about with one foot, one hand and one eye? Would they be lining up at the doors of our churches to join us in the pursuit of Christ?

Upon careful reflection, it is obvious that Jesus was speaking figuratively, saying something like this: *Remove the things which cause you to be tempted.*   Other passages of Scripture, from Genesis to Revelation echo this same message: Flee temptation! Do not hang around and toy with the very things that inflame your sinful desires. You will fall if you do. Instead, remove the sources of temptation and/or flee from the situations that are likely to cause you to stumble. In this way you can increase the likelihood that you will live a holy life in an unholy world, and maintain a testimony of integrity to a watching world. They will be attracted to Christ when they see you removing your sins, not when they see you removing your limbs!

We have chosen a rather drastic example to make our point. Yet, many key theological issues rest upon a proper assessment of figurative language in the Bible. Again, I cannot give you a detailed rule book for all of the figures of speech in the Bible. You must learn to exercise common sense. Think with care as you encounter Scripture that sounds figurative. Here again the value of commentaries is proven. A good commentary will point out figures of speech and explain them in light of the cultural context.

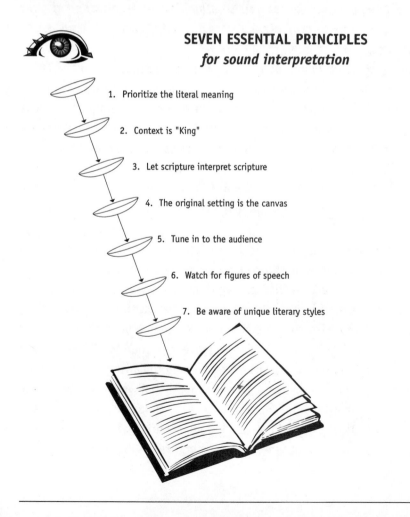

SEVEN ESSENTIAL PRINCIPLES
for sound interpretation

1. Prioritize the literal meaning

2. Context is "King"

3. Let scripture interpret scripture

4. The original setting is the canvas

5. Tune in to the audience

6. Watch for figures of speech

7. Be aware of unique literary styles

Reading Rule #7: BE AWARE OF UNIQUE LITERARY STYLES

We conclude our study of the rules of the read with a fancy word, *genre*. The word simply means "kind." The Bible is composed of various kinds of literature or different genres. Understanding the basic characteristics of the different genres can be a great aid in the interpretive process.

A daily newspaper has different genres. There is the front page, which differs in literary style from the comic section. You would not read the business news in just the same way that you would read the opinion page. The sports scores differ in style from the "Dear Abby" column. Have you ever noticed that when you read a full page article in the paper, and then find in tiny print at the bottom the words, "This is a paid advertisement," your interpretation of the entire article suddenly changes? That is because a paid advertisement differs in kind from an objective news article written by an independent reporter. The fact is that when you read the daily paper you are aware of this variety of genres. Your mindset changes automatically as you move from section to section reading and interpreting the paper.

In much the same way, the 66 books of the Bible contain a variety of genres of literature. It only takes a bit of work to familiarize oneself with these basic genres. Once we are familiar with biblical genres, we can read and interpret much more skillfully. I highly recommend the book by Gordon Fee and Douglas Stuart, *How to Read the Bible for All Its Worth*.[11] These authors identify and describe ten different literary genres in Scripture, giving guidelines for reading each.

For simplicity sake, we can summarize all biblical genres in four primary categories. Putting these four styles into a saying, you would have something like this: *Don't read a POEM like an EPISTLE nor a PROPHECY like a HISTORY.* Let us examine briefly the characteristics of these four biblical genres.

HISTORY: *Historical narrative* is one of the major literary styles of Scripture.   From Genesis to Esther, and from Matthew to Acts, you encounter historical narrative.   Since Genesis 3:15, the first promise of the defeat of evil, God has been at work in human history unfolding His plan of redemption.   From Genesis 3 to Revelation 21 we read the story of God restoring paradise.   Of course, the centerpiece of salvation history is the appearance of God Himself among us, redeeming us at His own expense in the person of Jesus Christ.   The four gospels and the passion story in particular, form the mountaintop of this salvation-historical narrative.

Essentially, you must read and interpret biblical historical narrative as a straightforward, reliable, factual record of events as they occurred.   Historical narrative material in the Bible is not fiction, myth or legend.   It is the real record of God's dealings with people in time and space, leading up to and then away from the cross of Calvary. These are real people and real events in real time.

Most biblical historical narrative consists of natural events (i.e., David moved from cave A to cave B).   The natural events are usually easy to grasp.   However, there are times in the historical narrative where God intervenes with a touch of the *supernatural* (i.e., God speaks to David through the mouth of a prophet, instructing him specifically to move).   When you encounter the supernatural in historical narrative, you must accept it as part of God's intervention in human history to advance His purposes and to reveal Himself to us.   There is no justification for the common practice of treating biblical miracles as non-historical, fictional material.   This amounts to an outright denial of the reality and

> *Bible history was not composed merely to inform but to transform the perspective of the reader. Thus, it is not a mere chronology of events; rather, it is a story with intention.*

presence of God and His sovereign right to act among us when and where He wants to. Allow God to act in historical narrative!

Another important characteristic of Bible history: *it is history packed with meaning.* Events have been carefully selected and arranged in such a way as to communicate important spiritual lessons. Bible history was not composed merely to inform but to transform the perspective of the reader. Thus, it is not a mere chronology of events; rather, it is a story with intention. Keep in mind, the Biblical history literature includes only a tiny fraction of events that occurred. We must assume that there were definite purposes governing the selection and arrangement of material.

The apostle John made it clear that he left out much of the life of Christ (John 21:25). That which he did record, however, he wrote with a careful purpose:

Many other signs therefore Jesus also performed in the presence of the disciples, which are not written in this book; but these have been written that you may believe that Jesus is the Christ, the Son of God; and that believing you may have life in His name (John 20:30,31).

Paul also was cognizant of the fact that Bible history was far more than simply dry, informative history.

For whatever was written in earlier times was written for our instruction, that through perseverance and the encouragement of the Scriptures we might have hope (Romans 15:4).

The careful student of biblical history, therefore, will develop an acute eye for themes and spiritual lessons imbedded within the historical narratives. The question must constantly be before us: What did the original author intend by selecting and arranging his materials in this fashion? Why does Matthew begin with the genealogy of Christ via the family of David? Why does Luke include a different genealogy than Matthew's, tracing Jesus' lineage all the way back to Adam, and why does Luke place the genealogy just prior to the beginning of Jesus' public ministry? Why does Mark chapter 2 contain a series of four questions, all of which seem to challenge the authority of Christ? Sometimes the answers to such intent-questions will be obvious, while at other places the author's underlying purpose is not as easy to discern. And sometimes we must allow for the simplest answer: the author is only intending to give the reader the facts of how an event occurred. In other words, the historical event is so important in and of itself, that the author wished to convey no other message than: It happened just like this!

Recall our earlier discussion of paragraph analysis. I said that when performing a paragraph overview on a narrative portion of Scripture, the final question you should ask is the question of *significance*. What is the point, the lesson, the warning, the theological intent of the historical narrative paragraph? Bible history is factual, real history and we must accept its stories at face value. Yet, it is history packed with meaning and we must read with an eye for themes. Once again, a quality book commentary will help you to discern narrative themes as they arise in a book. Since these underlying purposes and themes are usually not explicitly revealed by the authors, it is wise to compare your analysis at this point with the interpretation of others. It is unwise to ignore the historical-narrative themes. It is equally unwise to conjecture as to themes without good evidence. Study carefully, and consult other excellent students of the passage.

POETRY: *Hebrew poetry* is another major literary style found in the Bible. A large percentage of Job, Proverbs, Ecclesiastes, Song of Solomon and Psalms were composed in Hebrew poetry. The Hebrew prophetic literature also contains much poetic material. A basic understanding of the characteristics of Hebrew poetry will greatly aid your interpretation of these portions of Scripture

First, you can expect Hebrew poetry to abound with figurative language. When you read the poetical literature, therefore, put your figurative antennas up! You will encounter figures of speech on every page. For example:

Then the earth shook and quaked; and the foundations of the mountains were trembling and were shaken, because He was angry. Smoke went up out of His nostrils, and fire from His mouth devoured; coals were kindled by it. He bowed the heavens also, and came down with thick darkness under His feet. And He rode upon a cherub and flew; and He sped upon the wings of the wind. (Psalm 18:7-10).

This is David's very descriptive way of saying that God was his great warrior in life, coming to his aid when he was in trouble, bringing about mighty deliverances for him and routing his enemies. This is classic Hebrew poetry. It would be a mistake to press a literal interpretation on such figurative Hebrew poetry and to draw the conclusion that God *actually* has a nose with smoke pouring from it! Take another example:

Be gracious to me, O God, be gracious to me, for my soul takes refuge in Thee; And in the shadow of Thy wings I will take refuge, until destruction passes by (Psalm 57:1).

We are not to infer from this verse that God has wings. (If He did, why would He need to fly upon a cherub, or ride upon the wings of the wind, as suggested in the selection from Psalm 18?) Instead of picturing a God with wings, we are to see this as a figure of speech indicating God's loving protection for His child. He draws us under the umbrella

> *The chief characteristic of Hebrew poetry is parallelism. When you understand how this parallelism works, it will open up for you many lines of interpretation.*

of His protection, much like a bird would draw its young into the shelter of its wings. Hebrew poetry abounds with such figurative descriptions.

Another important characteristic of Hebrew poetry is that it does not have rhyme, but it does have rhythm. The chief characteristic of Hebrew poetry is *parallelism*. When you understand how this parallelism works, it will open up for you many lines of interpretation. I will illustrate below the three major forms of Hebrew poetical parallelism.

Synonymous parallelism occurs when the first and second lines say precisely the same thing, only in two different ways. Note the connective "and" between the two lines in the following verses:

O LORD, rebuke me not in Thy wrath;
And chasten me not in Thy burning anger (Psalm 38:1).

"Rebuke" parallels "chasten." "Thy wrath" parallels "Thy burning anger."

A fool's mouth is his ruin,
And his lips are the snare of his soul (Proverbs 18:7).

"Mouth" parallels "lips." "His ruin" parallels "the snare of his soul."

Synonymous parallelism basically gives you two looks at the same idea. The simple beauty of this is that when you find difficulty in understanding one line, chances are the parallel line will clear things up. Get in the habit of letting one line interpret the other.

Antithetic parallelism occurs when the first and second lines say opposite things, making a point by way of contrast. Note the use of "but" to sharpen the contrast:

A fool always loses his temper,
But a wise man holds it back (Proverbs 29:11).

"A fool" contrasts "a wise man." "Temper" stands opposite patience ("holds it back").

A man's pride will bring him low,
But a humble spirit will obtain honor (Proverbs 29:23).

"Man's pride" contrasts "a humble spirit." Being brought "low" contrasts obtaining "honor."

Antithetic parallelism shows you both sides of the issue. Again, by comparing line with line, you can better understand both of them.

Synthetic parallelism occurs when several lines build upon one another toward a climax. Psalm 1 begins with this kind of synthetic buildup:

How blessed is the man who...
1) does not walk in the counsel of the wicked,
2) nor stand in the path of sinners,
3) nor sit in the seat of scoffers.

But his delight is in the law of the LORD,
And in His law he meditates day and night (Psalm 1:1-2).

The first few lines combine together in synthetic parallelism (1,2,3) to describe what the blessed man does not do (note the progression, "walk," "stand," "sit"). Then, the next two lines set up an antithetic parallelism to describe what the blessed man does. Yet, instead of stating the contrast just once, it is repeated twice in synonymous parallelism. So you see all three kinds of Hebrew poetry at work in these 2 verses.

Hebrew poetry is very helpful, particularly when interpreting figures of speech, or when one line simply does not seem to make good sense. For example, you might have difficulty understanding what is meant by the following line:

A worker's appetite works for him.

That is actually something of a riddle, which is explained in what follows:

A worker's appetite works for him,
For his hunger urges him on (Proverbs 16:26).

Hunger is an incentive to work, so that the appetite can be satisfied. In a wider sense, unmet needs and desires can be a driving force behind productive activity.

When reading Hebrew poetry, therefore, watch for 1) the presence of figurative language and 2) the various kinds of rhythmic parallelism blended into line after line.

This morning I was reading Psalm 59. Notice the concluding two verses:

But as for me, I shall sing of Thy strength; yes, I shall joyfully sing of Thy lovingkindness in the morning, for Thou hast been my stronghold, and a refuge in the day of my distress. O my strength, I will sing praises to Thee; for God is my stronghold, the God who shows me lovingkindness (Psalm 59:16,17).

Now, consider these two verses as they are displayed in a simple diagram:

But as for me,
→   *I shall sing of Thy STRENGTH;*
→   *yes, I shall joyfully sing of Thy LOVINGKINDNESS in the morning,*
→   *for Thou hast been my STRONGHOLD, and a refuge in the day of my distress.*
←   *O my STRENGTH,*
←   *I will sing praises to Thee; for God is my STRONGHOLD,*
←   *the God who shows me LOVINGKINDNESS.*

This is like an antiphonal choir, one verse responding to or echoing the message of the other verse. In both verses David vows to sing praises to God and in both verses three words occur which describe God: strength, stronghold and lovingkindness. This is a perfect example of synonymous parallelism, blended with the use of figurative language (i.e. God is a "stronghold" or a safe place to hide from enemies). You will find innumerable gems buried in the Hebrew poetry sections of sacred Scripture. Work with it diligently.

PROPHECY: *Biblical Prophecy* is the third major literary style of Scripture. This style poses the most difficulty for Bible students for a number of reasons.

First, as with Hebrew poetry, the prophetic literature abounds with figurative language. It is sometimes difficult to decide where the figurative ends and where the literal begins. The Old Testament prophet Joel, for example, describes a horrible locust plague that swept into the land of Israel, devouring the crops and creating economic havoc. Joel uses this figure of the locust plague to describe the coming invasion of a fierce, devouring foreign army that will plunder the land as a divine judgment because of Israel's failure to obey the covenant with Yahweh.

As you read the book of Joel, it is difficult to know where the description of the literal locust plague ends and where the description of the invading army begins; the prophet has so thoroughly woven the figure into the entire fabric of his prophecy. This is, in fact, one of the interpretive challenges of this particular book, as any good commentary will point out to you. Yet, the message as a whole is very vivid and powerful: Israel will be judged for breach of the covenant, in accordance with the blessings and curses originally outlined in Deuteronomy 28. The invading army will leave Israel looking very much like a farmer's field after a locust plague: desolate! Yet, God in His faithfulness will come and restore His people after the period of discipline, and the mountains that were devastated in judgment will drip with sweet wine because of divine blessing.

The prophetic literature probably calls for the keenest eye for figurative language of any genre of Scripture. Impending judgments and future glories are almost always robed in heavily figurative speech.

A second cause of difficulty in reading prophetic literature comes in assigning specific historical time periods to the fulfillment of various prophecies. Is the prophet speaking of something that will be fulfilled in his own generation or is he pointing to a distant future event that will be fulfilled hundreds of years later?

It appears that even the prophets themselves struggled with this near-or-far question in understanding some of their own Spirit-given prophecies. As Peter said:

As to this salvation, the prophets who prophesied of the grace that would come to you made careful search and inquiry, seeking to know what person or time the Spirit of Christ within them was indicating as He predicted the sufferings of Christ and the glories to follow. It was revealed to them that they were not serving themselves, but you, in these things which now have been announced to you through those who preached the gospel to you by the Holy Spirit sent from heaven—things into which angels long to look (1Peter 1:10-12).

To further challenge the interpreter of prophetic material it appears that many times the prophets were touching upon near and far events simultaneously: i.e. pointing to an immediate event that would transpire in their historical setting, but this event would be a *foreshadowing* of some greater future event that would be the "ultimate fulfillment" of the prophecy. Some interpreters refer to this as the "dual fulfillment" of prophecy.

Thus, a prophecy of return from captivity leading into a time of blessing and prosperity might become, in the prophet's vision, a foreshadowing of the future Messianic kingdom when God would come among His people, purify them from evil and establish His reign visibly and dynamically on earth. Or again, a prophecy of invasion by the Assyrian army might have a more distant, ultimate reference: the end times "day of the Lord" in which God would come to the earth in a final, cataclysmic judgment and purification. Both the near and far events often overlap in one vision, the near event becoming a kind of prophetic springboard for the more remote event.

Again, the challenge can be illustrated from the prophecy of Joel. Take a look at Joel 2:28-32. You might recognize this passage because Peter quoted it in his message to Israel on the day of Pentecost (Acts 2). Was Joel pointing to the day of Pentecost only? Probably not. He was, most likely, referring both to the near term restoration that God would bring about in Israel after an invasion, and to the long term blessing of the outpouring of the Spirit on the day of Pentecost when God would begin to build a new kind of restored community for Himself.

This same kind of "dual perspective" seems to be present in Jesus' prophetic discourse from the Mount of Olivet (Matthew 24, Mark 13, Luke 21). Some interpreters feel that Jesus was speaking in this discourse entirely of the destruction of Jerusalem by the Roman army that occurred in 70 A.D. Another group of interpreters feel that Jesus was speaking entirely of the end of the age when at His second coming He will engage in a great battle against evil as the prelude to the establishment of His righteous rule on earth. A third group of interpreters, myself included, feel that Jesus is doing both of the above, in typical prophetic fashion. He is describing a near event, the destruction of Jerusalem in 70 A.D. At the same time, He is using this cataclysmic event as a prophetic springboard to prophesy of His second coming and the end of the age. The tribulation of Jerusalem, therefore, becomes a foreshadowing of the great tribulation that the whole earth will undergo just prior to the second coming of Christ. Both events, near and far, are woven together intricately in the prophetic message.

Yet another challenge in reading the prophetic literature has to do with the flow of thought. It is notoriously difficult to organize and outline prophetic literature, especially the longer Old Testament prophets. In fact, the synthetic reading process is most difficult in some of the prophets because the material seems to be disjointed, not flowing in any organized pattern.

In reading Jeremiah, for example, you will encounter dreams, visions, oracles, funeral songs, historical interludes, sermons, symbolic actions, etc. To add to this diversity, you will find that the prophet mixes his themes together in seemingly random order: judgment, blessing, disaster, future hope, invasion, Messiah. All are blended together instead of being neatly separated and organized. Further, the material in the book of Jeremiah is non-chronological in arrangement. You might be toward the end of the book and encounter a prophecy or a sermon that was chronologically prior to material earlier in the book. The book is, consequently, difficult to outline from either a logical or chronological perspective. The same challenge of outlining is seen when dealing with the New Testament book of Revelation. Eager prophecy students scour the book looking for a neat time line of end time events. They are typically frustrated, however, by the book of Revelation because it is notoriously difficult to figure out the flow of thought and the precise chronology of events.

The interpreter of Bible prophecy, therefore, must develop some skill in handling this unique genre. You must expect mixed themes and sudden leaps from the present to the distant future. You must watch for prophecies that have immediate historical relevance and, at the same time, distant fulfillments. And, as with the poetical material, you must have your figurative-language thinking cap on. The prophets are rich territory, often neglected by the average Bible student. Yet, the diligent student can, with some practice, become a capable interpreter of this material.

The best way to become familiar with the prophetic style is by reading the prophets themselves. I suggest beginning with some of the "minor prophets" before tackling the major ones. Try Joel, Micah, Haggai, or Malachi for starters. These will give you a good feel for the style and perspective of the prophets. Once you gain a feel for the prophets, you can tackle bigger projects like Isaiah, Ezekiel and Jeremiah. Daniel makes for a rather fascinating study, since it blends historical narrative with prophecy. Further, the prophecies of Daniel form a basis for understanding much of the New Testament prophetic material. Daniel, therefore, should be on your priority list for study.

EPISTLES: Epistolary literature accounts for the fourth major category of Biblical literature. In this category we find all of the New Testament letters from Romans to Jude. These epistles (Greek - epistole: a message, correspondence, letter) were the typical form of communication between persons or groups during the New Testament era. We should read them as if we were looking at a letter from someone else's mailbox.

> *These epistles (Greek - epistole: a message, correspondence, letter) were the typical form of communication between persons or groups during the New Testament era. We should read them as if we were looking at a letter from someone else's mailbox.*

Because the epistles are personal correspondence, they usually begin with a salutation and an introduction. The body of the letter follows, in which the writer sets forth the heart of his message. The epistles usually conclude with a list of personal greetings and then a closing benediction. These stylistic elements are present with exceptions in only a few of the epistles.

As with letters today, the styles of ancient epistles varied, depending upon the occasion that called forth the letter. Some epistles were highly personal (2nd Timothy) while others were more formal (Romans). One was firm in tone (Galatians), while another was gentler (Philippians). One letter sounded a note of imminent danger for people who were walking away from Christ (Hebrews), while another had a tone of sympathy for those who were suffering persecution (1Peter). In short, the epistles each have a style of their own, even though they are classified together as a genre. As you read and master each epistle, you will become quite familiar with the personality of each book.

> *The very complexities of sacred Scripture, which may seem daunting to the new student, create a depth and beauty which fascinate and challenge even the most advanced biblical scholar. Truly, God's Word is a deep, deep mine of precious ore!*

The epistles are generally much more logical and didactic than other forms of Biblical literature. For this reason, it is easier and safer to draw doctrine from an epistle than from a historical narrative, a poet or a prophet. You will find that the figurative language is much rarer in the epistles, giving way instead to straightforward, literal speech. The epistles usually come right out and directly state the matter, where the other genres often give you the truth indirectly or figuratively. It is, therefore, a good idea to master several of the New Testament epistles early on in your Bible study process, thus forming a solid foundation of theological understanding to serve as a basis for the study of other more complex genres of Scripture.

Summarizing this seventh rule of the read, we recall our little saying: *Don't read a POEM like an EPISTLE nor a PROPHECY like a HISTORY.* Be aware of unique literary styles in Scripture. Just as you would read the daily newspaper being aware of the presence of different styles, so you must get genre savvy as you work your way through books of the Bible. The very complexities of sacred Scripture, which may seem daunting to the new student, create a depth and beauty which fascinate and challenge even the most advanced biblical scholar. Truly, God's Word is a deep, deep mine of precious ore!

INTERPRETATION AND THE BIBLE STUDY PROCESS

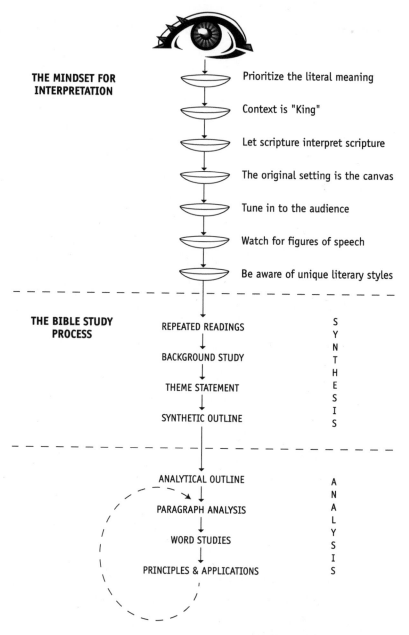

**THE MINDSET FOR
INTERPRETATION**

Prioritize the literal meaning

Context is "King"

Let scripture interpret scripture

The original setting is the canvas

Tune in to the audience

Watch for figures of speech

Be aware of unique literary styles

**THE BIBLE STUDY
PROCESS**

REPEATED READINGS

BACKGROUND STUDY

THEME STATEMENT

SYNTHETIC OUTLINE

S
Y
N
T
H
E
S
I
S

ANALYTICAL OUTLINE

PARAGRAPH ANALYSIS

WORD STUDIES

PRINCIPLES & APPLICATIONS

A
N
A
L
Y
S
I
S

CONCLUSION

I urge you therefore, brethren, by the mercies of God, to present your bodies a living and holy sacrifice, acceptable to God, which is your spiritual service of worship. And do not be conformed to this world, but be transformed by the renewing of your mind, that you may prove what the will of God is, that which is good and acceptable and perfect (Romans 12:1,2).

God in His infinite wisdom has chosen to reveal Himself to us in four ways: *Creation, Conscience, Christ* and *Canon.* Creation displays the grandeur of God. Conscience reminds us of the goodness of God. Christ manifested to us the unfathomable riches of the grace of God. And the Canon of sacred Scripture gives us the unfailing guidance of God. God has spoken. We must learn to listen.

Since the early days of my Christian journey some 30 years ago, I have been fascinated by the notion that God has put it all down in writing for me in the 66 books of the Bible; a Spirit-breathed library that I can study and understand for myself. The Bible is so simple that a newborn babe in Christ can open it and begin to drink the milk that produces growth. That was me, as a college student, when I began drinking in the book of Romans. Yet, the Word of God is so incredibly profound that a seasoned believer can find hidden treasures on every page. That is me, today, as I study and prepare to take my congregation through an intensive series on the book of Revelation. Wow! What a Book!

The great challenge facing today's Christian is that of *abiding patiently and consistently in the Word.* We are hurried in almost every aspect of our lives, and we are bombarded by stimulating information from other sources that keep us from logging time in the pages of sacred Scripture. Yet, the promise of Jesus is still true:

"If you abide in My word, then you are truly disciples of Mine; and you shall know the truth, and the truth shall make you free" (John 8:31,32).

It is the truth of God that sets us free and it is the practice of *abiding* (living, dwelling, remaining) in God's Word that takes us to the truth. We are set free to live as God wants us to live as we abide deeply in the precious Word of God. There never has been, and never will be, a short cut to spiritual transformation. The path to the transformed heart is the renewed mind.

Let the word of Christ RICHLY DWELL WITHIN YOU, with all wisdom teaching and admonishing one another with psalms and hymns and spiritual songs, singing with thankfulness in your hearts to God (Colossians 3:16).

My prayer for you is that you will have success in allowing God's Word to richly dwell within you; that you will experience a profound increase in your love for the Word of God and that your life will be transformed as your mind is renewed. I also pray that, as a result, you might live more fruitfully in the perfect will of God until the day when you meet the Living Word face to face in glory. Then, what we know in part and see dimly shall be replaced by a stunning vision of Christ. The days of abiding in the written Word shall give way to the endless day of abiding with the Living Word, and we will dwell in His glorious presence forever!

APPENDIX

Without a doubt the best way to develop skill in any area is to practice. The following material is designed to help you practice the various synthetic and analytical skills outlined in the preceding chapters.

I have chosen the book of 2nd Timothy for several reasons. First, it is a relatively short book. You will be able to master 2nd Timothy in a reasonable amount of time. Yet, in spite of its brevity, it will allow you to practice all the skills dealt with in earlier chapters. Second, it is a lively book. The background of 2nd Timothy, as well as its content, is very interesting. Once you immerse yourself in this little book, I think you will find it very captivating. Third, 2nd Timothy is very practical. There is hardly a book in the New Testament that more fully expresses the heart and motivation of the apostle Paul. This final letter from Paul, his last will and testament, is brimming with spiritual perspective and life-changing truth. All Christians can profit from the study of 2nd Timothy.

Following is a schedule of assignments that will take you through 2nd Timothy in about two months time. Also, you will find sample materials for the first chapter of 2nd Timothy. After you have done your own work, you may wish to compare your findings with mine.

Day	Assignment
1	Read 2nd Timothy.
2	Read 2nd Timothy.
3	Read 2nd Timothy.
4	Read 2nd Timothy.
5	Read 2nd Timothy and do background study on authorship.
6	Read 2nd Timothy. Put yourself in Paul's place as you read.
7	Read 2nd Timothy.
8	Read 2nd Timothy and do background study on recipient.
9	Read 2nd Timothy. Put yourself in Timothy's place as you read.
10	Read 2nd Timothy.
11	Read 2nd Timothy. Write a rough draft of the theme of the book.
12	Read 2nd Timothy. Write a rough draft of the synthetic outline of the book.
13	Read 2nd Timothy.
14	Read 2nd Timothy.
15	Read 2nd Timothy and do background study on the setting.
16	Read 2nd Timothy. Write second draft of the theme of the book.
17	Read 2nd Timothy. Write second draft of the synthetic outline.
18	Read 2nd Timothy.
19	Read 2nd Timothy.
20	Read 2nd Timothy and do background study on the purpose of the book.
21	Read 2nd Timothy.
22	Read 2nd Timothy. Write final draft of the theme statement.
23	Read 2nd Timothy. Write final draft of the synthetic outline.
24	Read 2nd Timothy chapter 1. Write rough draft analytical outline of chapter 1.

25	Read 2nd Timothy chapter 2. Write rough draft analytical outline of chapter 2.
26	Read 2nd Timothy chapter 3. Write rough draft analytical outline of chapter 3.
27	Read 2nd Timothy chapter 4. Write rough draft analytical outline of chapter 4.
28	Read 2nd Timothy chs.1 & 2. Refine your analytical outline of chs.1 & 2.
29	Read 2nd Timothy chs.3 & 4. Refine your analytical outline of chs.3 & 4.
30	Read 2nd Timothy from beginning to end!
31	PD 1:1,2. WS apostle. PA 1:1,2.
32	PD 1:3-7. WS sincere.
33	PA 1:3-7.
34	PD 1:8-12.
35	WS ashamed. PA 1:8-12.
36	PD 1:13,14. WS guard. PA 1:13,14.
37	PO 1:15-18. PA 1:15-18.
38	PD 2:1-7.
39	WS soldier. WS athlete. PA 2:1-7.
40	PD 2:8-13.
41	WS endure. PA 2:8-13.
42	PD 2:14-19.
43	WS handling accurately. PA 2:14-19.
44	PD 2:20,21. WS sanctified. PA 2:20,21.
45	PD 2:22-26.
46	WS repentance. PA 2:22-26.
47	PD 3:1-5. WS any word in 3:2-4.
48	WS any word 3:2-4. PA 3:1-5.
49	PD 3:6-9. WS Jannes, Jambres. PA 3:6-9.
50	PD 3:10-13. WS persecution of Paul at Antioch, Iconium and Lystra.

51   PA 3:10-13.
52   PD 3:14-17.
53   WS inspired. WS fully equipped.
54   PA 3:14-17. PD 4:1-5.
55   WS reprove. WS rebuke. WS exhort.
56   PA 4:1-5.
57   PD 4:6-8. WS drink offering. PA 4:6-8.
58   PO 4:9-18. WS Demas.
59   WS any name in 4:9-18. PA 4:9-18.
60   PO 4:19-22. PA 4:19-22.

Abbreviations:
PD = Paragraph Display
PO = Paragraph Overview
PA = Principles & Applications
WS = Word Study

SAMPLE ANALYTICAL MATERIALS

2nd TIMOTHY CHAPTER 1

Analytical Outline of 1:1-18

I. The Salutation 1:1,2
II. The Call to Faithfulness 1:3-18
    A. The opening charge 1:3-7
        1. Paul's thanksgiving for Timothy 1:3-5
        2. Paul's opening charge to Timothy 1:6-7
    B. Paul's faithfulness in suffering for Christ 1:8-12
        1. The charge to suffer 1:8
        2. The reason we should suffer 1:9-11
        3. The assurance within suffering 1:12
    C. Admonitions to be faithful to the Word 1:13-14
        1. The charge to retain sound words 1:13
        2. The charge to guard the treasure. 1:14
    D. The example of faithful Onesiphorus 1:15-18
        1. The many who deserted Paul 1:15
        2. The one who helped Paul 1:16-18

PARAGRAPH DISPLAY

2 Timothy 1:1,2

Paul is an apostle (messenger) of Christ. He received his commission by the will of God, not the will of man (see Galatians 1:11-17).

Paul
↓ ↓

   an <u>*apostle of Christ Jesus*</u>.
↓   ↓

   by the will of God
↓   ↓

The promise of life (eternal life) in Christ motivated Paul greatly in his life of service. This is an important note with which to begin this letter, as Paul is facing imminent death in Rome precisely because of his apostleship for Christ.
The promise of life holds him securely even in his final days.

   according to the promise of <u>life</u>
↓   ↓

         in Christ Jesus

↓
↓
↓
↓
↓

Timothy was no ordinary disciple of Paul. He was a special, beloved spiritual son. This letter is, in a sense, the passing of the torch from one spiritual generation to the next.

to <u>*Timothy*</u>
↓   ↓

   my beloved son

↓
↓
↓

The typical three-fold salutation of "grace, mercy and peace" is used. These three blessings come from God the Father and from Christ Jesus our Lord. Notice how tightly the Father and the Son are linked in the bestowal of divine blessings. Together they bestow grace, mercy and peace to us.

<u>***Grace, mercy and peace***</u>
↓   ↓
↓   ↓

   from God the Father
   ↓

   and (in company with)
   ↓

   (from) Christ Jesus our Lord

PARAGRAPH DISPLAY

2 Timothy 1:3-7

I thank God
   ↓   ↓

   ↓ *whom I <u>serve with a clear conscience</u>*

   ↓   ↓

   ↓   *the way my forefathers did*

   ↓

as I <u>constantly</u> remember you in my
prayers   ↓

   ↓   ↓

   ↓   *night and day*

   ↓

<u>*longing to see you*</u>

   ↓   ↓

   ↓   *even as I recall your tears*

   ↓   ↓

   ↓   *so that I am filled with joy*

   ↓

For <u>I am mindful</u> of the <u>sincere faith</u>
within you   ↓

   ↓

   ↓   ▶ *which first dwelt*

   ↓   *in your*

   ↓   *grandmother Lois*

   ↓   ▶ *and in your mother*

   ↓   *Eunice*

   ↓   ▶ *and I am sure it is*

   ↓   *in you as well*

and <u>for this reason</u>

   ↓

Paul thanks God for Timothy in his prayers. Paul serves God with a clear conscience (concerning his motives and actions which have led him into the present circumstances of persecution).

Paul prays night and day for Timothy. He longs to see him once again. He recalls Timothy's tears (at their last departure?) and knows there is a special love between them. Seeing him again would bring Paul great joy, but even in separation he is filled with joy as he remembers Timothy.

Paul is keenly aware of the quality of faith in young Timothy, a sincere faith that had been handed down to Timothy through several generations of godly women (note Acts 16:1). There were so many pretenders in Paul's day, so many with mixed motives and impure agendas. Timothy is truly in a different category. He is genuine.

Because of the quality of this young mans' character, Paul

I remind you to <u>kindle afresh the gift of</u>
<u>God</u>
    ↓   ↓
    ↓   ↓
    ↓   *which is in you through*
    ↓   *the laying on of my hands*
    ↓

for God has <u>not given us a</u>
<u>spirit of timidity</u>
    ↓.

  but
  ↓

(He has given us a spirit. . .)
of power
and love
and discipline.

exhorts him to rekindle the fire of his God-given potential for life and ministry. On a previous occasion, Paul had laid hands on Timothy and commissioned him into the ministry. Now, however, the time has come to renew this initial commitment and to stir into a fire the spiritual gift. Timidity is not the spirit which God has given to His servants (was this Timothy's natural disposition?); rather, God has given us a spirit of power, love and discipline. By the power of God's Spirit, Timothy can become all that God intended for him to become, in spite of natural inhibitions and in spite of the persecution that will surely be imposed upon him by the world.

PARAGRAPH DISPLAY

2 Timothy 1:8-12

Therefore (because God has not given us a spirit of timidity)
↓
↓ *do not be <u>ashamed</u>*
↓   ↓ *of the testimony of our Lord*
↓   ↓ *or*
↓   *of me His prisoner*
↓ *but (instead)*
↓ *join with me <u>in suffering</u>*
   ↓
   ↓ *for the gospel*
   ↓
   ↓ *according to the power of <u>God</u>*

↓
who has <u>saved</u> us and <u>called us</u>
   ↓   ↓ *with a holy calling*
   ↓ *not according to our works*
   ↓ *but (instead)*
    according to <u>His own</u>
    <u>purpose and grace</u>
     ↓
     ↓ *which was granted to us*
     ↓ *in Christ Jesus from all*
      eternity
     ↓ *but (in addition)now has*
      been <u>revealed to us</u>
      ↓

Since God has empowered us to live boldly for Him (v.7), we must not be ashamed of either the gospel message or of those who carry His message, even if the messenger is a prisoner (of the Lord, "His prisoner" not Rome's prisoner!).

We should be willing to suffer for the gospel (main theme of this paragraph). God will supply the power we need to endure the suffering He calls us to.

The God for Whom we are willing to suffer is the One who called us to Himself in eternity past. The salvation we now enjoy came to us not as a result of our good works but because of God's own purpose and grace that He granted to us.

God's purpose and grace was granted to us in Christ in eternity past, but these became visible and real to us when Christ appeared on earth and revealed them to us.

Christ Jesus put an end to the power of death (a great thought for someone who might soon be

by the appearing
of our Savior
<u>Christ Jesus</u>
↓

↓
↓ *who abolished death*
↓ *and (in addition and contrast)*
  brought life and immortality <u>to light</u>
        ↓ *through <u>the gospel</u>*
              ↓

↓
for which I was <u>appointed</u>
    ↓ ▶ *a preacher*
    ↓ ▶ *and an apostle*
    ↓ ▶ *and a teacher*
    ↓
For this reason <u>I also suffer</u> these things
    ↓
    but (even so)
    ↓
    I am not ashamed
    ↓
    for (the reason)
    ↓
    I know whom I have believed
    ↓
    and (with this knowledge)
    ↓

put to death!). He brought life
and immortality to light
through the good news (which
concerns His death, burial and
resurrection for us).

It is this gospel of eternal life,
which Jesus brought to light,
for which the imprisoned Paul
was appointed a preacher, an
apostle and a teacher.
The preacher proclaims the
truth boldly. The apostle (key
messenger) gives special
leadership and authority to the
movement of the message. The
teacher instructs people
carefully in the doctrines
associated with the message.

Paul is willing to suffer without
shame for this noble
appointment, and he is calling
on young Timothy to abandon
shame and fear and to be
willing to suffer, if necessary,
for the progress of this glorious
God-given message of eternal
life.

In the face of suffering, Paul
fixes his hope on the One whom
he knows (he has a firm grasp
on the character and
trustworthiness of God).

Paul is convinced that God will
not somehow lose track of his
life and his circumstances.
Instead, God will guard Paul's
life carefully, overseeing the
outcome of every trial, every
situation, until that day which
God has fixed for Paul to
complete his mission and to

***I am convinced that He is able
to <u>guard</u>***

↓────────────

↓

what I have entrusted to Him
↓

until that day

meet the Lord face to face. The Lord will have His way with Paul, and will ultimately bring him safely home to His heavenly kingdom (ch.4:18).

PARAGRAPH DISPLAY

2 Timothy 1:13,14

Retain the standard of sound words
↓   ↓   ↓
↓   ↓   *which you have heard from me*
↓   ↓
↓   *in the faith and love*
↓   ↓
↓   *which are in Christ Jesus*
↓
↓
↓
↓

Retain . . . Guard! This passage looks like the kind of synonymous parallelism one might find in Hebrew poetry.

Retain the standard of sound words (truth) that I have taught to you, Timothy. Retain this truth as you live in the realm of the faith and love that are in Christ Jesus.

Guard the treasure
↓   ↓
↓   *which has been entrusted to you*
↓
↓

through the Holy Spirit
      ↓
     who dwells in us

Guard the treasure (of divine truth) that has been entrusted to your care. Guard this truth (from any form of opposition) as you live in the realm of empowerment of the Holy Spirit who lives within us.

PARAGRAPH OVERVIEW

2 Timothy 1:15-18

SETTING

Who: Paul, the prisoner; Onesiphorus, a believer from Ephesus (note 4:19) who had been an encouragement to Paul more than once; Phygelus and Hermogenes, two men who turned away from Paul in his hour of need (nowhere else mentioned in Scripture); "all who are in Asia" - the Christian community in the region of Ephesus in Asia Minor.

When: Paul was in prison in Rome. The day of his execution was drawing very near. Onesiphorus came to visit Paul during this difficult time in the apostle's life.

Where: In a Roman prison that was cold and uncomfortable.

EVENT

What: The day of Paul's execution was drawing near. He did not know how much time he had left. Most of his Christian friends had deserted him at his first trial (4:16 compared with 1:15). There was a great stigma attached with the imprisoned apostle and most people were not willing to bear the shame of being associated publicly with him. Paul's spirit was strong, but this imprisonment undoubtedly took a great physical, mental and emotional toll on him. In the midst of this, Onesiphorus eagerly searched for Paul and found him. Once he found Paul he "refreshed" him. He had previously ministered to Paul in some significant way when Paul was in Ephesus. What a wonderful sight the face of Onesiphorus must have been when he showed up at the prison that day! Paul was very thankful for his concern and pronounced a blessing on Onesiphorus (1:18), asking that the Lord reward him for his service.

SIGNIFICANCE

Why:
1. Onesiphorus exemplifies what Paul has been talking about thus far in his letter: bold, unashamed dedication to the cause of Christ, regardless of the consequences. He stands in stark contrast to the many deserters who turned away from Paul in his hour of need. Onesiphorus exemplifies the "faithful man" (2:2) who will be the subject of most of chapter 2 in this letter.

2. Onesiphorus sought active ways to minister to God's chosen servant. The time and the place did not make much difference to Onesiphorus.   Whether Paul was imprisoned in Rome or fighting spiritual battles at Ephesus, Onesiphorus was ready to move in to encourage and refresh Paul. Paul was, undoubtedly, in need of such personal encouragement at this hour.

Word Study on "Apostle" - 2nd Timothy 1:1
General Usage: The word *apostle* literally means "sent one," being derived from two words, *apo* = "from" and *stello* = "to send." The basic idea is that of a "messenger;" one who has been commissioned to carry a message from one person or group to another. In a technical sense, the word applies to that select group of disciples who were eyewitnesses of the risen Christ, who then carried the message of His resurrection to the world. The word is also used in a broader sense, however, of other key leaders in the New Testament churches (e.g. Barnabas, Acts 14:4,14; Andronicus and Junias, Rom.16: 7; Epaphroditus, Phil.2: 25).

Usage in context: In reference to Paul, the title "apostle" is used in the technical sense. He is one of that select group of individuals who was permitted by God to see the risen Christ, and then Paul was commissioned in a special way to carry the message of salvation to the world. Particularly, Paul was the "apostle to the Gentiles," being called by God to bear the message of Christ to the non-Jewish world. His title as an "apostle" is attached to the beginning of most of his letters, though not all. He sometimes omits this title when others wrote with him (e.g. Phil.1:1; 1Thess.1:1; 2Thess.1:1). This title carries a distinct note of authority. It gives the impression that the letter that we are about to read is a message from God; that it is, penned through the hand of Paul.

Principles & Applications from 1:1.2
Principles
1. All of us who know the good news should consider ourselves as 'messengers' of that news.
2. The promise of eternal life should motivate us to pour out our lives for Christ.
3. We should cultivate "beloved son" relationships in the process of discipleship.

Application
I have been casually helping John in his walk with Christ for several months now, but I haven't really made the effort to develop the kind of in-depth relationship like Paul had with Timothy. I will seek to cultivate a "beloved son" kind of relationship with John by spending more personal time with him each week. I will try to get to know his interests and needs and be more intentional in the things I try to build into his life. I will pray that God gives us a unique 'Paul-Timothy' kind of relationship.

Word Study on "Sincere" - 2nd Timothy 1:5
General usage: The word *sincere* is *anupokritos* in Greek. It is translated "genuine," "sincere," "without hypocrisy." The latter

translation brings out the idea of the original word best. The word *hupokrinomai* was used to describe actors on the stage who were "pretending" to be somebody they were not in reality. The word *anupokritos* means, therefore, "non-pretending" or "non-play acting." It speaks of someone, or something that is "the real thing." It is used to speak of genuine faith (1Tim.1:5; 2Tim.l:5), genuine wisdom (James 3:17), and genuine love for one another (2Cor.6:6; 1Pet.1:22; Rom.12:9).   Generally, anupokritos depicts an inward reality that matches the outward actions.

Usage in context: Paul uses this word to describe the faith of young Timothy. It is a "for real" faith; it is a faith that means business. In the historical context there were many "disciples" who were falling away from the faith and forsaking Paul in his imprisonment. Times were tough for Christians in that day. It was not easy to stand firm for the Lord.   But Paul sees in Timothy a pure, genuine, non-pretending faith in God. He sees this as the basis for Timothy's future leadership potential.   Timothy was not playing games; he was not acting out a phony Christian life. His faith was not hypocritical.

Principles & Applications from 1:3-7

Principles
1. We must serve God with a clear conscience.
2. We should always be striving to cultivate a "for real" (not hypocritical) faith.
3. Parents are to reproduce a sincere faith in the lives of their children and grandchildren.
4. We should constantly be rekindling the spiritual gift that God has given to us.

Application

I will take some new initiatives to cultivate the faith of my children. I will search for some materials that we can study together in order to deepen our faith. I will set some specific goals for our progress in learning together, and I will take more personal responsibility for their spiritual growth and development.

Word Study on "Ashamed" - 2nd Timothy 1:8,12

General usage: The word *ashamed* is *epaischunomai* in Greek. The preposition epi makes this a strengthened form of *aischumo* (shame). The basic idea in epaischunomai is that of "intense shame." It is used in the New Testament to describe the shame one might feel in association with the gospel message (Rom.1:16; 2Tim.1:8, 12;), with the Lord Jesus and His words (Mark 8:38), or with those who are suffering for the cause of Christ (2Tim.l:16). It is also used to describe the shame one might feel when thinking about past evil acts (Rom.6:21).

Usage in context: In 2nd Tim.1:8-12 the main idea is that of willingness to suffer potentially intense shame (epaischunomai) for the gospel of Christ. Paul commands Timothy (v.8) not to be ashamed "of the testimony of our Lord" (the gospel message), "or of me His prisoner" (the gospel messenger who was presently in prison). In v.12, Paul uses himself as the example of one who was unashamed to suffer for Jesus Christ. In a later paragraph (1:15-18) Paul will cite Onesiphorus as another outstanding example of one who was unashamed of the stigma attached with the gospel message, and especially of the potential shame associated with Paul, the imprisoned gospel messenger.

Principles & Applications from 1:8-12

<u>Principles</u>

1. We must not be ashamed of the message or the messengers of the gospel of Christ.
2. We must be willing to suffer for the gospel by the power of God.
3. God's eternal purpose, not our works, is the source of our salvation.

<u>Application</u>

I have been afraid to share my faith with others because I am fearful of what they might think of me. Basically, I have been ashamed of the gospel message. I will, by faith, lay aside this shame and I will begin to pray for and seek opportunities to share the gospel with my friends, relatives and neighbors. I will look for opportunities to tell people my own story of my faith in Jesus Christ.

Word Study on "Guard" - 2nd Timothy 1:14

General usage: The word *guard* is *phulasso* in Greek, which means to "watch over." It is translated "guard," "keep," "maintain," "observe" and "protect." In Luke 11:21 it is used of a man protecting his household against robbers. In Acts 12:4 and 28:16 it is used of soldiers who were guarding Peter and Paul. It is used by Paul in 2nd Tim. 1:12 to speak of the protection which God provides for His servants until the day He desires to take them home to be with Him.

Usage in context: In 2nd Tim.1:14 the idea seems to be that of "protecting" the treasure of sound doctrine against false teachers and others who might attempt to distort the truth. Phulasso in this context seems to be nearly synonymous with the verb "retain" in the previous verse (1:13). The two commands seem to be saying the same thing in two slightly different ways: Hold on to the sound teaching; Protect the treasure of truth.

Principles & Applications from 1:13,14

Principles

1. We should hold tightly to the sound doctrine that we have been taught.
2. Sound doctrine must be maintained with a combined attitude of faith and love.
3. By the power of the Spirit we should protect the truth against distortion.

Application

I need to become better grounded in the basic doctrines of the Christian faith. I will obtain a good book on Christian doctrine and read it over the next few months. I will ask my pastor this week if he can recommend a good book on this subject. I will set aside one hour per week to accomplish this study.

Principles & Applications from 1:15-18

Principles

1. The real test of faithfulness comes when we are called to take a stand for Christ.
2. We should be eager to minister to God's servants whenever they are in need.
3. The service we render today will be richly rewarded when we meet the Lord.

Application

I will minister to the missionaries from our church this month. I will get the names and addresses of our missionaries from the chairman of the missions committee. Then, I will write each of them a personal letter of encouragement. I will also ask each of them if they have any needs that I can meet.

NOTES

Preface
1. Dallas Willard, *Renovation of the Heart: Putting on the Character of Christ* (Colorado Springs: NavPress, 2002), pp.104,5.

Chapter Two
1. Cited in *Halley's Pocket Bible Handbook* (Chicago: Halley, 1943), p.557.

Chapter Three
1. Robert A. Armstrong, *Mastering the Books of the Bible* (New York: Thomas Y. Crowell,1916), p.23.
2. James Gray, *How to Master the English Bible: An Experience, a Method, a Result, an Illustration* (Chicago: Moody Press, 1951), p.24.
3. Gray, p.29.
4. Howard F. Vos, *Effective Bible Study* (Grand Rapids: Zondervan,1956), p.25.
5. G. Campbell Morgan, *The Study and Teaching of the English Bible* (London: James Clark & Co.), p.37.
6. The first four of these guidelines were advanced by James Gray (*How to Master the English Bible*) and were later adopted by Herbert Lockyer, *All About Bible Study* (Grand Rapids: Zondervan, 1977).
7. Gray, *How to Master the English Bible*, p.38.
8. Morgan, *The Study and Teaching of the English Bible*, p.35.

Chapter Eight
1. Robert A. Traina, *Methodical Bible Study: A New Approach to Hermeneutics* (Wilmore: Traina, n.d.), p.170.
2. *Webster's New Collegiate Dictionary*, 1981 ed., s.v. "context."
3. James W. Sire, *Scripture Twisting: 20 Ways the Cults Misread the Bible* (Downers Grove: InterVarsity Press, 1980), p.52.
4. Milton S. Terry, *Biblical Hermeneutics* (Grand Rapids: Zondervan, n.d.), p.231.
5. Traina, *Methodical Bible Study*, p.94.
6. Alfred Edersheim, *The Life and Times of Jesus the Messiah* (Grand Rapids: Eerdmans, 1971).

7. Craig S. Keener, *The IVP Bible Background Commentary, New Testament* (Downers Grove: InterVarsity Press, 1993).

8. Louis Berkhof, *Principles of Biblical Interpretation* (Grand Rapids:Baker,1950), pp.124,125.

9. J. Robertson McQuilkin, *Understanding and Applying the Bible* (Chicago: Moody Press, 1983), p.137.

10. Terry, *Biblical Hermeneutics*, p.247.

11. Gordon D. Fee and Douglas Stuart, *How to Read the Bible for all its Worth: A Guide to Understanding the Bible* (Grand Rapids: Zondervan, 1981).

Jubilee Publishing

ORDER FORM

E-mail Orders: www.jubileepublishing.com

Mail Orders: Mail this completed form with your payment to Jubilee Publishing, 41079 Concept Drive, Plymouth MI 48170

☐ Please send _____ books at $12.95 each (plus shipping-see below)

☐ Please send more information about Jubilee Publishing

Name: _____

Address: _____

City: _____ State:_____ Zip:_____

Telephone: _____

E-mail address:_____

Sales Tax: Please add 6.0% for products shipped to Michigan addresses.

Shipping by Air:
U.S.: $4.00 for first book; $2.00 for each additional book.
International: $9.00 for first book; $5.00 for each additional book (estimate)

Payment: ☐ Check   ☐ Money Order   ☐ Credit Card
            ☐ Visa   ☐ MasterCard   ☐ AMEX   ☐ Discover

Card Number: _____

Name on Card: _____ Exp. Date:_____